Reign of Terror 1940

Reign of Terror 1940

'REIGN OF TERROR' 1940

THE PHRASING IN THIS BOOK PORTRAYS IN DETAIL THE TERRIFYING AIR RAIDS BY THE ENEMY ABOVE TO TRY AND EXTINGUISH THE MORALE OF THE BRITISH PEOPLE.

ISBN 978 1 9160587 8 1

Published by: Percychatteybooks Publishing

© Percy W Chattey 2019

Percy W. Chattey has inserted his right under the Copyright, Designs and Patents Act, 1988, to be identified as the author of this work.

All rights reserved

This book is sold subject to the condition that it shall not by way of trade or otherwise, be lent, resold, hired out, or otherwise circulated without the publishers prior consent in any form of binding or cover other than that in which it is published this also includes electronic transfer to a third party without a similar condition including this condition being imposed on the subsequent purchaser.

Reign of Terror 1940

STORY TELLING TWENTY ONE

Acknowledgments
As always my gratitude to my lovely wife Jean, friend and soul mate, who has helped with the editing and all rewrites, also listening to all my ramblings whilst putting these articles together.

My appreciation to the following
In no specific order

Derek Cook for the cover

Trudie Oakley for the poem on page one

Richard Seal

Chris Wyatt

William Riddiford

Caroline Goss

Clive Adlam

Bob Thomas (RIP)

Kenneth Webb (RIP)

Lucy Patricia Boby

Reign of Terror 1940

Content

Suffer Little Children	4
Authors Note	5
Early Events	6
The Blitz	9
BBC News	11
The Phoney War	13
Churchill	23
War	24
William Riddiford	25
Balham, London	48
Civil Defence	50
Where bombs dropped	51
Sheffield	52
Churchill Speeches	59
Ninety Year Old	61
Coventry	66
Bob Thomas	75
Hull	83
Blackmoor	88
Liverpool	107
Innocence of Children	114
Birmingham	120
Important Targets	125
Portsmouth	126
Annelies Franks	130
A New Horror	133
The Enigma Machine	141
The V1 & V2	144

Reign of Terror 1940

This reflective verse by Trudie Oakley, the words are so true as it did happen during the 'Reign of Terror 1940' in the towns and cities of the United Kingdom.

Suffer Little Children

The children scramble through the man made hell
Their once happy home now a rubble strewn shell
Their father is dead and their mother defiled
Why is the happening - Why are they exiled

Dust covered they scurry from one hole to another
They have to move on but must also find cover
The shelling has stopped but they know not for long
Yasmin wants to cry but she has to be strong

Surely someone can save them - can keep them from harm
She dreams of a haven that's cosy and warm
The bombing begins - there's much more in store
One bomb finds their shelter – the children are no more

Destruction is wanton with no end in sight
Will nobody help these poor folk in their plight
The pilot looks down at his work – smiles - nods his head
He thinks of his children home safe tucked in bed
He's followed instructions he's done a good job
His conscience is clear – and be praised for what he begot

Authors Note

In the following writings we present and describe true stories of events, detailing the deprivation and the horror of children and their families living through the period of the Blitz, by the bombing by the German Luftwaffe over the United Kingdom.

This was the period in the early part of the 1940s when the four countries in the fortress island of Britain, (but for short forays in the 1914 - 18 war), for the very first time in their history were severely bombarded and attacked internally by a foe from the air, causing severe damage across the Realm to each of its major cities and towns.

These are true personal stories told by those who lived through this period recalling the scars imprinted on their minds, as they agonized at the time, cowering in their air raid shelters praying their family and loved ones would stay safe, all the time listening to the onslaught of carnage raining down around them from the enemy above,

Reign of Terror 1940

Early Events leading to the Terror of 1940.

The lead up to the Second World War is well documented and can be traced back to the earlier part of the 1930s. Prior to this period, and after the Great War of 1914 - 1918, Germany became the Weimer Republic and struggled with Political control and the economy. Whilst this is a very limited history of this period it led to the great recession which started in the late twenties and continued with hyperinflation.

It was in 1928 when the Nazis won only 12 out of 600 seats in the Reichstag and Hitler was widely regarded as a funny little man who ranted and raved like crazy in public!

However, the German economy was more exposed to short-term borrowing than any other in Europe in the 1920s, and the effects of the Great Depression caused an almost permanent political crisis from 1930 onwards.

At this time the country was largely ruled under emergency powers (in other words, by decree). Germany was already deeply divided between Left and Right, and this division rapidly intensified.

By late 1932 many politicians felt that the political structures were deadlocked and that something drastic had to happen to continue the process of government. On the advice of the German Nationalists (the DNVP) and some others, President Hindenburg invited Hitler to form a coalition government of Nationalists and Nazis.

At the time it was assumed that the Nazis were the junior partners in the coalition. Within a few weeks Hitler upstaged the DNVP, established a dictatorship (March

Reign of Terror 1940

1933) and two months later Germany became a one-party state.

When Hitler gained power, the economy stimulated, and many jobs were provided. Hitler began working at stopping any possible internal threats and slowly began encouraging the discrimination of the Jewish people. After which he began invading and captivating surrounding countries, many were previously held territories by Germany but were lost after the first World War.

Hitler's territorial demands grew and grew, even though he made promises to end them. These countries were under-developed and didn't stand a chance. Some of them just gave up, and as in the case of Austria, cheered the invaders more like a parade than a new occupying force.

The British and others were trying to negotiate with him to stop the expansion of Germany. Hitler was told if he continued to invade adjoining countries then the Allies would see that as an act of war.

Hitler took little notice and ordered his Panzer tanks into the country of Poland, which although was largely inferior, decided to strongly oppose Hitler and even mounted their small and ancient armies. However, Poland fell to the invading forces.

As the Allies had warned if he took this step then War would be declared and as his tanks rolled into the Polish countryside in September 1939 the Second World War became a reality.

Reign of Terror 1940

Daily Express Headline September 3rd 1939

"The Battle of France is over, I expect the Battle of Britain is about to begin"
Prime Minister Winton Churchill 1940.

The Blitz

The Blitz *was the sustained bombing of Britain by Nazi Germany between 6 September 1940 and 10 May 1941. The Blitz hit many towns and cities across the nation, the main onslaught began with the bombing of London for 76 consecutive nights. By the end of May 1941, over 43,000 civilians, half of them in London, had been killed by bombing and more than a million houses were destroyed or damaged in London alone.*

London was not the only city to suffer the Luftwaffe bombing. We describe how other important military and industrial centres, such as, Birmingham, Coventry, Sheffield, Liverpool, and Hull, all suffered heavy air raids and high numbers of casualties.

To the North of the country in Scotland the worst of these attacks was the Clydebank Blitz, which took place on March 13th and 14th 1941. It was considered to be the worst case of destruction and civilian deaths in Scotland

Reign of Terror 1940

during the war. The two nights saw 528 people dead and a further 617 residents seriously injured.

Isa McKenzie, speaking when she was 88, was only 12 years old when the attack took place. Looking back, she called it two nights of 'constant bombing'.

The town was well established with approximately 12,000 houses and tenement buildings, but by the end of the blitz only seven of these stood undamaged.

In the rest of the United Kingdom there were only two places which had little damage. Oxford, as it was understood that when Hitler invaded and took over the country, he wanted to use this fine city as his Headquarter, the other Blackpool, to be used for recreation purposes for his troops.

Reign of Terror 1940

BBC News Broadcast September 1940

London blitzed by German bombers The German Air Force has unleashed a wave of heavy bombing raids on London, killing hundreds of civilians and injuring many more. The Ministry of Home Security said the scale of the attacks was the largest the Germans had yet attempted. "Our defences have actively engaged the enemy at all points," said a communiqué issued this evening. "The civil defence services are responding admirably to all calls that are being made upon them."

The first raids came towards the end of the afternoon, and were concentrated on the densely populated East End, along the river by London's docks. About 300 bombers attacked the city for over an hour and a half. The entire docklands area seemed to be ablaze as hundreds of fires lit up the sky. Once darkness fell, the fires could be seen more than 10 miles away, and it is believed that the light guided a second wave of German bombers which began coming over at about 2030 BST (1930 GMT).

The night bombing lasted over eight hours, shaking the city with the deafening noise of hundreds of bombs falling so close together there was hardly a pause between them.

'REIGN OF TERROR' 1940

An actual note made at the time of an air raid by:
Major Trevor Middleton Wyatt,
Royal Artillery

Reign of Terror 1940

The Phoney War

Percy Chattey

By the spring of 1940 the War had been in place for more than six months and hostilities had not spread to the home front. Life had continued normally although there were restrictions, some food rationing and people were persuaded not to travel. Signs everywhere saying, *'Is your journey really necessary?'* About that time in May of that year, our troops were being rescued from Dunkirk. This event has been well documented in history when ships, and boats of all sizes, set off across the English Channel to rescue more than three hundred thousand men from the beaches of Western France

Evacuation

One night, when I was not quite four, I was woken up at about midnight and told to get dressed, so I got out of the warm bed into a bitterly cold bedroom. I was frightened, I did not know what was happening and thought perhaps the Germans had arrived. It was just as cold downstairs as the fire in the living room, although still glowing from the previous evening was not giving out very much heat. Outside it was pouring with rain and still dark and we could hear the noise the deluge of water was making outside the house.

Leaving home with my elder sister by three and half years, accompanied by both our parents we had to walk in the wet for about a mile to Whalebone Lane Senior School, where many years later I was to become a pupil.

In the playground were a line of cars, their engines running giving out a low growl and the smack, smack noise of the windscreen wipers sweeping back and forth. There were a group of children all lined up carrying gas masks, boys in one line, wearing coats and short trousers with socks and shoes, the girls with similar footwear in another line but wearing dresses or skirts with coats over. We were all given a brown cardboard tag to tie on a lapel or button. I was too young at reading, so I do not know what it said but it was some form of identification.

After a little while, by now soaking wet because of the continuous rain, we were directed to the cars. I remember

being somewhat disappointed because I was put in a similar car to the one my father had owned, and when I had sat in it beside Nan's house, a Ford 8 or it could have been a Morris, they looked similar. I really wanted to go in the big car, the one in front of the one I was told to get into, but other children were put into it.

There were tearful goodbyes to the parents and the cars started off in convoy and out of the gates. Inside the Ford/Morris it was cold and damp, the windows misting over with all our breathing and the damp clothes we had on. Basic vehicles did not have the luxury of heaters, that was still a few years away. As we drove along the driver was keeping the inside of the windscreen clear by wiping the moisture off with a cloth.

Reign of Terror 1940

I was now going further than I had ever been before in my life, but worse it was with people I did not know and none of us had any idea where we were going or why. The cars hummed and rattled their way, going South, although at that time I did not know the meaning of the word.

It was murky and shadowy, each vehicle had coverings over their headlights so that the light would not spread and be seen from the air. There were no streetlights, the shops and houses were in total darkness in compliance with the Blackout Laws. The rain was pouring down steadily making the journey very dark and slow.

We arrived at the Ford Motor Company in Dagenham, driving through the factory gates and down to Fords Jetty which was built into the River Thames as seen in the picture with a ship tied up alongside it. I remember it was very gloomy with deep shadows and a low hum emanating from the giant motor works. The cars stopping beneath large cranes and we were told to get our things and to line up. Years later I was to drive on to that jetty many times.

As I have said it was very black as outside lights were not allowed, because of the danger of enemy bombers lurking overhead. We held each other's hands as we were ushered onto a vessel; I do not know what sort of boat it was and was probably more of a ship, as by now I was too distressed and exhausted to take in what was going on. It must have been very early in the morning when we left the jetty as it was still dark.

I do not remember much of the journey which would have been quite long going down the Thames and round the Essex and Suffolk coasts, because we finally arrived in Norfolk. I was not to know that at the time, it could have been anywhere, and nobody was saying anything about our location. By a combination of train and bus we eventually arrived at a small

Reign of Terror 1940

coastal village, Cromer, early in the hazy morning light, where we lined up on the side of the street. Total strangers came along the line looking at the name tag and picking children and taking them away. (*Can you imagine that happening today?*)

I was near to last to be chosen and taken to a small, terraced cottage near a railway bridge that crossed the road. I was very disappointed because other children had gone off in pairs, and I was on my own. I do not remember very much other than the lady was nice. If she had a husband, he was probably away at the war.

The thing that really struck me when I arrived was the small front room with the front door opening straight onto the street. Which I thought was very strange. There was a tall cupboard door in the living room, again I was surprised because when she opened it the stairs started immediately, ours at my home in East Road, Chadwell Heath had a passage and a front door before you got to the stairs.

Reign of Terror 1940

We went up to the next floor and she showed me what was to be my room which had a window overlooking the road, I did not like it; my personal things were still back in my bedroom at home.

I also remember being totally traumatised by being taken away from where I had been brought up, not understanding what was happening and why I was living in this strange house with no family and a bedroom which was nothing like my one at home. For some reason the period I spent in Norfolk, is not very clear, I don't think I was very happy, strange people with a weird brogue, I felt out of place and badly wanted to see my parents.

Although by now the war had been in place for over a year and the evacuation seemed a bit pointless. After about six months or so, I was told that I was being sent home this time by train. And I did that to be met by my father when I arrived at a large railway station in London.

It was many years later, when I thought about that period, I could not understand why we were sent to Norfolk by boat, when there must have been an immense risk that the Germans could have attacked the ship and sunk it. Sadly, this did happen to a liner which was taking children to be evacuated to Canada, with the loss of most of the people on board.

During the evacuation period I do not remember where my elder sister Fran was, she was in the line with the girls and must have been sent away at the same time as me, but I do not remember, and I do not know where she went.

Reign of Terror 1940

I Return Home from Evacuation.

The first thing I noticed, when I arrived back home in East Road, Chadwell Heath from the evacuation, was all the trees spaced along both pavements had been taken down and the road had been widened. The surface finish was in white concrete instead of the more pleasing black tarmac, which it had been when I left. This changed the whole nature of the road from a little back water to an area waiting for something to happen.

I was told this was because if Whalebone Lane, which ran parallel with it, became unusable by a bomb destroying it, then the traffic could be diverted through our road to go to the important docks in Dagenham, my thought at the time was *'but we have not seen any bombs.'*

By that time Ford Motor Company was making military vehicles and the factory had been converted to war work, so there was a need to keep routes to these important facilities open. The use of our road as a diversion never happened but at times the bombs fell not far short of making it a possibility.

One day when I came home from school a large hole had been dug about halfway down our garden. I was told it was for the Anderson shelter, a couple of men were still there with their picks and shovels finishing off the work.

The next day this silver corrugated iron oval thing stood out of the hole and the last of the steel sheets was being bolted to the front, leaving a small opening for the entrance which was down a few steps formed in the earth out of the surrounding ground. It was then that I was told, so as to protect the shelter against bomb blast it needed covering with the earth that had been dug out of the hole. So, for the next hour or so at the age of about five that was my job.

Reign of Terror 1940

An Anderson Air Raid Shelter

Before the war, a day out was to go pea picking. At about a mile from our house there was a farm in the north part of Whalebone Lane. It was always just getting light when we would arrive very early in the morning and climb onto the back of a lorry, there were no seats in it and we would hang out over the side as it travelled to its destination which would be a field awaiting to be harvested. On arrival we would alight from the vehicle clutching our lunch in a bag with sandwiches and a thermos flask of tea, which Mother would have put together that morning.

Once off the lorry everyone would be given a sack and shown to a row of peas or some other produce, for picking. When one filled the sack, it was taken to the farmer who would weigh it on a large set of industrial scales, and then he would make payment determined by the weight of the sack. As a small boy I was never very good at it, but Mother was very quick and filled the hessian bags speedily.

Reign of Terror 1940

In its wisdom the War Office turned this farm into an Army camp with an Ack-Ack gun facility. Half round corrugated Nissan huts were built for accommodation, after which a Regiment of the Royal Artillery moved in, there were also dining rooms, offices and guard rooms with all the paraphernalia which the Army brings with it.

Away from the buildings, and in the fields where vegetables had been grown before the war, and where we used to go pea picking, gun emplacements were built surrounded by sandbags, a simple and quick method designed to deflect the blast from exploding bombs, so that the guns could continue to operate and fire at the enemy planes.

Ack Ack guns being installed in a field

The Army, to boost morale at a time when there was nothing happening war wise and to keep the troops happy who were in most cases many miles from home and loved ones, they would hold parties in the camps canteen inviting local people to mix with men who served there. Soldiers that could play a musical instrument would form a band and while the parents partied and danced, we children were confined to a small room, because we were not allowed in the area where alcohol was being served, that was totally illegal.

Reign of Terror 1940

A little bit further away another large area had been taken over and converted to an airfield which was to become the very famous Fairlop Aerodrome, a fighter plane station where Spitfires and Hurricanes were based; it was one of the many airfields they flew from in the Battle of Britain.

Not too far away in Dagenham were the vast docks where imports and exports went through. There were also different factories making various items all dedicated to the war effort. Fords Motor Plant built everything from engines to complete

Part of the docks in East London - the River Thames, with ships tied up alongside it is running diagonal across the page on the right.

cars and lorries. The large Dagenite Batteries plant which manufactured vehicle electrics. Beckton Gas works producing gas from coal to supply the factories and households.

This area of water was vast, and still is, making them the largest enclosed docks in the world with an area of 250 acres (1 km$^{2)}$. If the land facilities is included for loading and unloading ships that would make it four times greater. As a matter of interest building started in 1880 and finished in 1921.

Nearer to home was the Goodmayes Railway Marshalling Yards in East London. This was one of the largest in England at that time, where rail trucks carrying war material were shunted into the right order behind a rail engine, to be taken to their destination which could be anywhere around the country.

All these facilities the enemy would want to destroy, and they were all within a few miles from our house. Not that it occurred to me at the time, but it must have been something that my parents thought and worried about.

~~~

Reign of Terror 1940

"We shall come through."

*"When I look back on the perils overcome
And on the mountain waves in which the
Gallant ship has driven, when I remember
All that has gone wrong and remember all
that has gone right, I feel sure that we have no
need to fear the tempest. Let it roar, let it rage,
we will come through".*

Extract from Prime Minister Winston Churchill Speech in 1941

WAR

*This famous picture looks strange, milk being delivered amongst all the rubble and bomb damage.
Life had to go on and it is possible he is supplying a mobile refreshment unit set up for those helping in finding survivors as in the left background of the picture.*

Reign of Terror 1940

The Civilian Force

In September 1940 the Government started to collect and collate information relating to damage sustained during bombing raids. This was known as the 'bomb census'. Initially, only information relating to London, Birmingham and Liverpool was collated but by September 1941 the bomb census had been extended to cover the rest of the UK.

Its purpose was to provide the government with a complete picture of air raid patterns, types of weapons used, and the damage caused – in particular to strategic services and installations such as railways, shipyards, factories and public utilities.

Besides the Armed Forces other units were being created, The Home Guard. There were also units formed nationally called ARW (Air Raid Watch sometimes known as Air Raid Wardens),

William Riddiford seen here in more relaxed times was a member of the ARW and was stationed in Dagenham. William kept a diary of the actions during the Blitz detailing events, number of planes, bombs dropped and the damage they caused.

We have been

privileged to use some of them in this account and they follow at suitable intervals. The earlier ones although ready for the enemy to attack it was not until after September 1940 did the onslaught begin.

They are written by the author at the time of the incidents, sometimes a little disjointed and with spelling mistakes which underlines the stress he was under.

The original was in pencil and has been converted by Barking and Dagenham Borough Council where they were displayed, and it was they who converted them into print as seen here.

From Riddiford's Diaries.

Saturday August 31
Take Cover warning 8.25am-9.05a. Nothing heard. Off Duty.
Take Cover warning 10.40am-1 1.20am
Off Duty. Heard a little machine gun fire.
Take Cover warning 1.00pm-2.00pm
Off Duty. Very quiet. Only heard a drone of planes, probably our own.
Take Cover warning 5.50pm-7.15pm
Off Duty. Saw crowds of planes in Dagenham Dock direction. A mass of AA Gun smoke. Heard planes howling & moaning & diving at the Germans. No bombs dropped near. Hornchurch & Elm Park heavily bombed. Railway hit. Taking passengers from Dagenham Station to Upminster Station by buses. Two parashoots in skie being shot at by

Reign of Terror 1940

Home Guard, our own airmen. One went overhead, came down in Merry Fiddlers yard, Beacontree Heath. Dad & I rushed up on our cycles.
Take Cover warning 10.00pm-10.25pm
Off Duty. Nothing heard. A few single planes raiding. Heard bombs in distance.
Take Cover warning 1 1.25pm-12.00pm
Off Duty. The sixth raid warning. Single plane & small group raiding. Nothing here.

The expansion of the London Underground Railways was not complete at the start of the war. In the 1930's it was still being extended when the London Central Line of the arrangements was being developed out to Hainault in Essex. At the start of the war in 1939, the tunnels and the stations on this enlargement were complete in the sense of building work but there were no rail lines or plant in place. The Plessey Company, which made radio parts and other electronic systems, had a modern factory on the Eastern Avenue, not far from the East Road junction. To protect the work, they were doing for the war effort, a lot of their manufacturing was moved to the tunnels of the incomplete rail network, where they would be safe from enemy bombing.

The semi completed station at Redbridge near Wanstead in East London was part of the new unfinished line and became an air raid shelter. People would go down the many steps - as the lifts were not operational, with blankets, pillows and food for supper to spend the night away from the risk of being caught out when the German planes were overhead.

I remember before the shelter in our garden was built, we went to Redbridge Station on a number of nights, it was a long way from where we lived, a bus ride along the Eastern Avenue. On one occasion after a night trying to sleep in the cold of the

Reign of Terror 1940

tunnel on the hard ground while some men were making a fair amount of noise playing cards, and I think Dad was amongst them, we made our way up the steps of the proposed station. When we arrived in the open, we were told there had been an air attack overnight which had resulted in no buses running. There was no choice and we had to walk the three miles or so home. Carrying the blankets and other items we had taken to make the night as comfortable as possible. I do not think we went again after that.

The picture is of people sheltering in an unfinished underground railway station, making themselves comfortable for the night where the rail tracks will eventually be laid. The platform is on the right and in the distance the circular entrance to the tunnels can be seen with a row of lights in it.

Reign of Terror 1940

In the front living room at East Road where we lived, there was a long, tall heavy sideboard, made of hard wood, it was against one wall, with mirrors along the top and an opening below about two feet square along its length. In front of it and taking up most of the middle of the room, was a big rectangular heavy wooden table. Instead of the long trip to Redbridge, beds were made under the furniture as protection if the worst should happen.

The summer of 1940 crept past with the odd air raid otherwise there was little activity from the skies in the area where we lived. It was known that the Germans were preparing landing barges on the East coast of France for an invasion across the English Channel. In the cinemas the Pathè News showed pictures of these landing barges lined up adjacent to the French Ports. This brought a new fear to the people.

From Riddiford's Diaries

Wednesday September 11 1940

Take Cover warning 1 1.45am-12.15pm On Duty. Very quiet. 3.20pm—4.30pm
Very heavy A.A. gun fire followed a group of enemy planes up river. A trail of white puffs of smoke left in the skie.
Take Cover warning 5.15pm-5.30pm On Duty. Very quiet here.
Take Cover warning 8.40pm-5.37am
On Duty. Another All-night single raiding planes but many in various districts at same time. The heaviest A.A. gun fire yet. Almost a continuous barrage all night long, shells bursting many districts at same time like twinkling bright stars. Could hear shrapnel falling. Dad found 5 pieces. Myself 4. Big fire at midnight seen in Woolwich and R.A. Docks direction. Very clear moonlight night. One of the driest summers on record.
90 enemy planes down. 24 of ours. 9 pilots safe.

Reign of Terror 1940

In that period twenty million tons of food a year was being imported into England to feed a population of forty-six million people. The German forces targeted the ships heading for the U.K., and in the early part of the conflict were doing a lot of damage to our supply routes.

To help overcome the losses the 'U' Boats were causing, the Ministry of Food issued every person with a Ration Book limiting the amount of food one could buy. To obtain one of these the populace had to register at one shop to receive their supplies. The ministry would provide the shop with enough food for those people registered with it. The ration book itself contained coupons which could only be used on the date marked on it, which controlled the amount of provisions required in the system.

Most bread at that time was baked by small local bakers. To help in stopping wastage the Ministry decreed bread could only be sold a day old, the reasoning being new uncut bread, that is how a loaf was normally made, was too fresh to cut thinly and when fresh it was too tasty, and people would eat too much.

Historians looking back at this period are convinced that if Hitler had used this time to attack the U.K, Germany could have won. Instead, the Government was given months of grace which allowed our defences and armed forces to become stronger.

This all changed in September 1940. There had not been an air raid for a long time and we had got used to staying in the house in the evening. We were sitting at home when the air raid warning sounded. At first, not a lot of notice was taken; there had been a lot of trial runs and testing of the systems before that night. It had been quiet for so long we did not know that this was the start of Hitler's determination to bring Great Britain to its knees.

Reign of Terror 1940

From Riddiford's Diaries

Friday September 13 1940

Take Cover warning 7.30am-8.30am
On Duty. Fairly quiet here. Heard gun fire in distant. Bomb dropped Four Wantz, Dagenham.
Take Cover warning 9.45am-2.00pm
On Duty. Heavy cloud & rain. Single raiding planes. Five [or fire] bombs on Buckingham Palace. King & Queen in residence. Gun fire at intervals
Take Cover warning 4.15pm-4.30pm
On Duty. Very quiet here 9.00pm-5.40am
Another all night raid. Single & small group plane raiding. Terrific gun barrage. Clear moonlight skie. Dad & myself went shrapnel gleaning in the moonlight. Dad found 20 pieces, one piece 100zs. Myself 4 pieces. Bombs dropped Hedgmans Road, 7 in front of Sterling works. About 100 house roofs damaged at Hedgmans Road. Many houses damaged in the district by shrapnel.

When the guns started firing from the Army camp we knew it was for real. We could hear the gunfire from the *'Ack-Ack'* guns which indicated the enemy planes were not very far away. There was not a lot of time as we could hear bombs being dropped so with mother and baby Bob, I squeezed in the cupboard under the stairs; many weeks before that Mum had cleared the bedding from under the sideboard convinced that no planes were ever coming. Dad and Frances, my sister were under the big solid wooden table in the front room.

At first, I think we all thought it would be over very quickly and although we were uncomfortable it was bearable, but it was not to be. It was a long time in that cramped space waiting for the noise to stop and the 'all clear' to sound. Even today,

31

Reign of Terror 1940

as I write this, we were recently watching a feature on the television about the blitz all those years previously. In the programme there was the sound of an air raid warning, my heart did a little flutter, and I had a brief moment of fear.

The following early evening it was quiet, and we were preparing for bed, when a lot later than the previous day, the sirens started their wailing, and the guns were firing once more. We left the comfort of the house in our night clothes to go to the air raid shelter in the middle of the garden. After the stay in the cupboard of the evening before, a lot of effort had gone in to get it finished during the day so that we could sleep there.

The total floor area of the interior of the Anderson was not much larger than a normal size double bed, and the floor was about a metre below ground level. Even as a five-year-old I had to duck my head to get in the entrance. When we first arrived, it was dry and there was a small round oil stove with a blue flame on the floor to give some heat. But oil stoves give off moisture which did not help with the condensation problem.

On both sides of the shelter narrow wooden bunk beds had been constructed against the walls. '*Beds*' is a poor word for them as they did not have any form of springs just a wood covering beneath a very thin mattress. On each side there was one on the ground with another above, and a small one going across the rear wall for baby Bob to sleep in.

There were no windows only the small opening for the door, which had a blast protecting wall of sandbags on the outside in case a bomb fell nearby. The theory was the wall would redirect the blast away from the shelter. The internal walls were smooth galvanised corrugated iron curving over into an arch with no through ventilation. With five people breathing plus the oil stove - the cold walls and the roof soon became extremely wet with condensation, the water running down in rivulets onto the blankets and bedding. There was no door on the entrance way which allowed some air to enter the confined space, but it was freezing air especially in the winter months. Not very comfortable for sleeping, it was very damp and cold and another problem was when it rained the floor would get very wet.

From Riddiford's Diaries.

Wednesday September 18 1940
Take Cover warning 7.00am-7.30am
On Duty. Very quiet here. Lovely bright morning.
Take cover warning 8.30am-8.50am Off Duty. Slight gun fire.
Take Cover warning 9.35am-10.20am
Off Duty. Battles overhead between RAF & the enemy.
Take Cover warning 1 1.35am-1 1.45am
Off Duty. Very quiet here. I was on allotment digging potatoes.
Take Cover warning 12.55pm-2.30pm
Off Duty. Still on garden. Many planes overhead. I counted 60. The skie was a mass of lines & rings made of smoke or vapour made by the planes. Patchy cloud. Heard no bombs.
Take over warning 4.20pm-4.45pm Off Duty. Very quiet here
Take Cover warning 5.15pm-5.55pm
Off duty. Heavy cloud. Heard drone of planes. Slight gun fire Rainham direction
8.05pm-5.40am Off Duty. Another all night raid, the eight warning for the day. Heavy gun fire again all night. Heard two bombs screaming coming down, some fell in Hitherfield Road 200 yards from away. Houses damaged. 48 enemy planes down in the day raids.

Reign of Terror 1940

It was extremely traumatic for us children. There was no set routine. During the day going to school on your own, and it did not matter if it was raining or even snowing you still went, looking up into the sky as you did so to see if any planes were lurking around. Sometimes it was possible to hear gunfire or bombs dropping in the distance.

An Anderson shelter after a bombing raid

At first the feeling was that the bombing and the nightly raids would soon stop, but they didn't. For a five-year-old a night is a long time, a week a lot longer but a month is an age. But imagine the raids becoming a nightly occurrence, going on for month after month, lack of sleep, the constant fear of wondering when and where the next explosion would be. The sheer terror - not only in the nights but to hear a plane during the day would set your heart beating.

The German aircraft very rarely called during the daylight hours, but occasionally the warnings would sound and then if you were out and about it was a matter of running to the nearest shelter. These had been built by the authorities,

Reign of Terror 1940

normally tall, (*well I was only small*) brick structures with flat concrete roofs on the side of streets. Once inside you stood with others who had been caught in the open and waited for the 'all clear', and that could be a very long time.

There was a report of an air raid shelter in central London which could hold 400 people and of a similar construction as described above. This shelter, because of its size had a ventilation shaft a few feet in diameter going out through the roof. By sheer bad luck a German bomb entered the shaft and exploded in the shelter killing the people inside.

Shelters did protect against the blast of these terrible weapons, but we were all aware in the event of a direct hit they were little protection. In Dagenham a few of the shelters were hit with a bomb, all that remained afterwards was a large crater some remains of the shelter scattered around but no sign of the occupants.

Another item which was common to see on the side of the road was large black steel water tanks twenty to thirty feet in length and probably about six feet wide. Beside them fixed to brackets were stirrup pumps, these were similar to bicycle pumps, with a hose which was put in the tank and another to point at a fire in the hope of putting it out. These tanks were about five to six feet tall and on hot days we would climb into them for a swim. The authorities stopped this pleasure by putting wire netting across the top.

There were also lines of large concrete square blocks which would stretch in rows in areas where it was deemed, if the enemy landed on our shores and advanced inland, then it was hoped these large blocks would slow the movement of their tanks. Beside the concrete structures were large steel angle irons to fill the gaps between them so as to block the roads if the need arose.

Reign of Terror 1940

From Riddiford's Diaries.

Friday September 20 1940

Take Cover warning 1 1.00am-12.00am
Off duty. Slight gun fire. Many planes heard. Fairly quiet here.

Take Cover warning 7.55pm-12.30am

Off Duty. Dad and myself just heard 5 minutes of the 9 O'clock news, then we rushed back in the shelter because of heavy firing overhead when there was several terrific bangs and bits of stone and dirt was falling on the garden and on the greenhouse. We were frightened to come out for a few minutes because of delayed action bombs, then we heard a lot of shouting in the road. We came out and the path and road was smothered with dirt and stones. A bomb had dropped about 80 yards away in a back garden, near a shelter, no one hurt. Another about 45 yards, in the road, in front of the big gates of the school playground shattered the roof of the black house, damaged Barritts shop roof, big crater in the road, flung kerb stones over the house and into the playground, no one hurt. Another in Bonham Gardens in between 4 shelters. 22 people in the 4 shelters, one boy slight head injury, about 130 yards. Another about 150 yards Valence Wood Road. Delayed action, several houses evacuated, had not gone off by Sunday 22nd.

Another 150 yards Warrington Road smashed 3 houses down to the ground, no one hurt, people in their shelters. Another about 400 yards Lymington School playground.

Another about 500 yards Bartons Bakeries, 12 hurt.

Reign of Terror 1940

One of the saddest sights of that time was after an air raid to see a house that had taken a direct hit which would just be a pile of rubble. The properties close to them would also be damaged and it was not uncommon for a side wall of a dwelling to have been destroyed, leaving rooms complete with furniture suspended in the open on a sloping unsupported floor, with small personal items scattered about. I remember one such place with the bedroom on the first floor looking as if it had been untouched by the event with a pristine made up double bed.

When father had been *'called up'* for war service in the Army, Mother did not expect to see him until the conflict ended. But he had always suffered with stomach problems and was discharged from the forces as being unfit. How or why, he started working on the docks I do not know, but no doubt as an electrician he would have been ordered to carry out work in the London Docks helping in the repair of war damaged ships.

It was about ten- or twelve-mile cycle ride, each way, maybe more which he would do twice a day, and on arriving home after a brief meal he would be ready to attend the local Home Guard Centre for duty. He would stay out at night, as an ARW with others as a look out for unexploded or firebombs which were being dropped, also to be of assistance if anything happened.

From Riddiford's Diaries.

Monday September 23 1940
Take Cover warning 10.00am -10.50am On Duty.
Take Cover warning 5.35pm—6.05pm On Duty. Very Quiet here.
The Kings speech during the raid. [all night warning]
On Duty. Very heavy A.A. gun fire all night.

Reign of Terror 1940

Incendiary Bombs dropped all round us. One 8 yards from the shelter, one on the lawn in the school. One fell through the school stores roof, on to a chair in the stores. Dad smashed the windows, put sand & dirt on them, one fell 15 yards from our house, in front of the library, one fell through an house & started a fire, land mine fell near Civic Centre. Landmine in Brenwood Road. shattered several streets of their doors & windows. Crater about 30 feet deep killed 17, blew shelters to bits.

Every night was the same routine, we would put coats on over our night wear and make our way down the garden and huddle together in what was to become known as '*The Dug Out*'. The air raids would start after dark and go on for hours as we lay on the bunks listening to the ceaseless drone of the bombers overhead, hearing the bombs whistling out of the sky, wondering each time where they were heading. Some explosions were just a crump in the distance, other times a lot nearer, the noise so loud, the ground and the shelter violently shaking, we would be convinced our house had been hit. Sleep was not possible, sometimes just dozing when there was a lull in the war that was raging outside, all the time feeling very cold

In the years leading up to the war with Britain, the Germans had used a method known as Blitzkrieg (*lightning war*) to invade other countries. When Hitler had made a decision with his Generals of the nation they wanted to invade and conquer, then they would put a well-established and successful invasion technique in place. Their method was to send hundreds of bombers to drop heavy bombs on the countries cities and defences to bring the people into submission, so that when their ground forces followed this bombardment there was very little fight left in the country they had invaded.

Reign of Terror 1940

With the horror their powerful forces could inflict from the air, which they used to demoralise the populous before the start of their attack, most of Europe had no answer and were quickly overrun by Hitler's troops. It was now our turn, starting with the air raids.

Children in the East End of London made homeless by the random bombs of the Nazi night raiders, outside the wreckage of what was their home September 1940

The nearby Army camp with its *'Ack Ack'* fire power had various other guns. Beside the loud noise of the standard guns there was one we nick-named *'Big Berther'*, when it fired there was a loud bang and the ground seemed to shake, what it was used for we never knew.

In between times, the *'Pom Poms'* would be going off in fast sequences. It was a gun that could fire shells in quick succession, some of which would be tracers. A tracer is like the lighted tail of a rocket firework going high into the air showing the gunners where their shells were going. The search lights would be piercing the night sky looking for the enemy, when one was found the tracers would search it out so that the shells following would make a hit.

Reign of Terror 1940

From Riddiford's Diaries.

Sunday September 29 1940

Take Cover warning 4.15pm—5.00pm On Duty. Very quiet here. Take Cover warning 8.10pm—6.00am On Duty. One of the largest bombs dropped in Grafton Rd at 11.15. Went out on job: terrible sight 3 Anderson shelters blew 80 — 100 yards away, Also parts of bodies 60 — 80 yards away. Bomb crater about 30 feet deep & about 45 yards round. 4 people killed. Shelter blew off one family, and they finished up sliding down the crater, unhurt, marvellous escape. About 150 houses damaged, gas leaking water running etc., raid still on overhead & heavy gun firing. Went out at day break picking up pieces of flesh with shovel & sack.

Through all this we lay in the shelter very quietly, no one saying a word, just listening to the thundering noise, hoping Dad was alright, wondering and wishing it would soon stop. But the months were to roll by and the German planes were intent on doing as much damage as they could. For 176 consecutive nights, or six months I have since read, they continued their bombardment night after night.

Each morning after the beautiful sound of the single note of the siren giving the *"all clear"*, we would leave the safety of the Anderson shelter. The enemy rarely came during the daylight hours. Scattered around the garden and in the streets would be pieces of shrapnel that had dropped out of the sky, the remains of the shells that had been fired from our guns, sometimes a piece of aircraft among them.

As winter approached the war rumbled on in all its intensity.

Reign of Terror 1940

The sky every night lit by the tracers from the *'Pom Poms'*, search lights weaving across the dark sky, white smoke caught in their light as the *'Ack Ack'* shells exploded high in the air. The flashes from the exploding shells lighting up the sky, also the silver-coloured Barrage Balloons swinging on their steel cables, tethered at a few hundred feet to stop low flying enemy aircraft from strafing the ground.

Above it all was the sound and the drone of engines from the bombers, their bombs screaming down, with explosions and gun fire from the local Army camp. Sometimes it was possible to be able to distinguish the lighter sound of the fighter planes as they swooped in the sky searching out their prey. Amongst all this the bombers would drop flares on parachutes to light up the ground so they could see the targets they wanted to aim at.

From Riddiford's Diaries.

Saturday October 5 1940
Take Cover warning 2.17am — 3.40am Off Duty.
Heavy gun fire at intervals. Take Cover warning 11.25am — 11.55am On Duty. Slight gun fire.
Take Cover warning 2.00pm — 2.30pm. On Duty. Slight gun fire heard drone of planes, many vapour marks in the skie made by high planes.
Take Cover warning 4.1 0pm — 4.45pm On Duty. Fairly quiet here. Take Cover warning 7.30pm — 6.30am On Duty. At 1 1.40 a very large bomb dropped in Windsor Rd, in the road shattering about 200 houses also Charlecote Rd School.
Also 25 minutes later an high explosive bomb fell in Thompson Rd on many shelters. 18 killed & 6 missing, we

Reign of Terror 1940

were called out, also all squads leaving the depot empty. Terrible job, people blown everywhere, working in the dark, shops shattered at Five Elms.

In the early 1940's I started attending the Warren Secondary Modern School, which was in Whalebone Lane, and was for boys only. Girls had another section to the rear of the property that part was strictly out of bounds to us lads. As stated earlier, Whalebone Lane was part of the main route to the docks, which are on the banks of the deep waters of the river Thames, along with the Ford Motor company. Frequently from the school playground, we would see, convoys of military vehicles going south, sometimes rows of Jeeps other times lines of lorries or amphibious DUKW all going towards Dagenham, and no doubt the facilities offered there.

It was one sunny afternoon when walking home from school, when I heard an engine noise of a plane, and then gun fire, it was a little way away. This continued for some time, probably less than a minute but it seemed longer. The people out in the open were lucky if they did not get hit as there had been no air raid warning for them to take shelter. I learned

Reign of Terror 1940

later that it had been a German Messerschmitt, a fighter plane, which had flown low over Chadwell Heath High Road, strafing the road with its machine guns, making two passes causing casualties and damage. The last time I was in Chadwell Heath, about forty years after the end of the war, some of the bullet marks were still there on the side of the buildings that had survived the years.

Who would do such a thing, mowing down women and children as they went about their daily lives? Children being collected from the nearby junior school, while other mothers/grandmothers as they shopped in the many stores to be found in the High Street. Did the pilot think it was a game shooting up an area with no military involvement, or was he instructed to do so from a higher authority?

On one occasion they bombed the Beckton Gas works. The result being there was no gas in the house to cook with. So meals were heated over the open fire, even this was a problem as coal was in short supply and people would look for and sort out different types of fuel to keep the fire alight to cook on at meal times and to keep warm during the evening.

There was no fixed pattern, sometimes just as it got dark there would be an air raid warning. Other times, when the family

Reign of Terror 1940

were convinced the enemy were not coming, sitting warm around the fire or getting ready to go to bed, the familiar sound of the air raid warning would be heard. We would look at each other and it was off to the cold, damp, musty shelter.

The raids also varied in intensity. Some nights the action was in the distance, nearer the city of London where the Docks were. other nights the Luftwaffe, (*German Air Force*), would concentrate their efforts closer to our home, the airfield at Fairlop, the factories and docks in Dagenham, and a little nearer to home the railway marshalling yards at Goodmayes. When these places were their targets the noise would be deafening with the smell of cordite and burning in the air.

On the odd occasion during the evening, Dad wearing his Army issue tin hat, would look in through the small opening of the shelter, exchanging a few words of comfort with mother. One evening when the raid was particularly harsh, he came rushing to the dugout. With no time for an explanation he insisted Mum follow him, we lay there fearfully, wondering what was happening.

After a while Mum returned and explained, a German airman whose plane had been shot down, had drifted down and landed in the street a few doors down from our house. The panic was to share the silk from the parachute. The risk of bombs and shrapnel falling, all being ignored as our neighbours shared out the material amongst themselves. Where the plane crashed or of its remains I do not know, nor what happened to the airman.

I also do not remember what happened to the silk material of the parachute or if it was of any use to the new owners. The excitement in the street was because any form of cloth was in short supply and could only be bought if your coupon ration was adequate. Something dropping out of the sky was not to be scoffed at. What I do remember is Mum was very good on

Reign of Terror 1940

a sewing machine and maybe she made something out of it.

I would just like to add, over the years since the war, a lot has been said about the damage the Allies caused to German cities during the bombing that was inflicted later in the conflict by British and American air forces, especially to Dresden – I would agree, in as much it should not have been.

However, on the other hand how do you fight a dictator who had, since the nineteen thirties, destroyed many cities, not only ours but others, and had murdered millions of people and hundreds of thousands in nightly bombing raids? On a later page is a picture of what he achieved in one night in Coventry. The German Forces participating in that kind of damage, to countless towns and cities across Europe, not forgetting the one hundred and seventy-six continuous nights they destroyed the third of the housing stock in London. Did the German Reich really believe they were not vulnerable to similar reprisals?

One of the worst problems that the home front had during the period of the German bombing was the shortage of resources and man power to deal with the damage as it was happening. The Palace of Westminster, (*House of Commons*) was bombed fourteen times during the blitz. During the night of 10/11th May1941 the bombers were back again and many incendiaries landed on the roof of the building. The fire-fighters were outnumbered and there was not enough equipment to pump water to cope with the flames. Their choice was either to try and save the Commons Chamber where Members of Parliament debated, or the more ancient Westminster Hall. They went for the latter. The Chamber was destroyed and finally rebuilt but not completed until 1952.

St Paul's Cathedral in London was hit many times throughout the blitz and the many months of continuous bombing. The volunteers posted on the roof did a valiant job of dowsing the

Reign of Terror 1940

many incendiary bombs that were dropped on the building.

This picture is of the famous St Paul's Cathedral, London, after an air raid. The picture was taken by Herbert Mason on 29th December 1940 from the Daily Mail building and was published two days later

It has often been said that it is a wonder a lot of churches survived as if they were being looked after by a power above, it could also be said about other land marks like Tower Bridge in London. But I have a different theory I think they survived because the bombers used them as markers to identify other more important targets; without radar in their planes, these tall buildings in cities and towns would confirm their location and no doubt lead them to their proposed destination.

By this time the tide of war was turning and everyday there would be flights of Allied Bombers darkening the skies as they made their way on bombing missions against the enemy. The familiar drone coming from the planes of our Air Force was comforting and so very different to the noise of the German ones. We would stare skywards counting the craft as they flew past. They would go out in strict formation. It would be hours later when we would watch the survivors struggling back in ones and twos as they made their way home, some with smoke gently pouring into their slip streams.

St Katherine's Docks in East London after a night time raid in 1940

Reign of Terror 1940

Balham,
London

The Disaster at Balham Tube (Subway) Station. During the Second World War. Balham was one of many deep tube stations designated for use as a civilian air raid shelter. At 20:02 on 14 October 1940, a 1400 kg semi-armour piercing fragmentation bomb fell on the road above the northern end of the underground facility, causing a large crater into which a bus then crashed. The northbound platform tunnel partially collapsed and was filled with earth and water from the fractured water mains and sewers above, which also flowed through the cross-passages into the southbound platform subways, with the flooding and debris reaching to within 100 yards of Clapham South. According to the Commonwealth War Graves Commission (CWGC), sixty-six people in the station were killed - although some sources report 68 - and more than seventy injured. The damage at track level closed the line to traffic between Tooting Bec and Clapham Common, but was repaired rapidly with the closed section and station being reopened on 12 January 1941.

Reign of Terror 1940

From Riddiford's Diaries.

Friday November 15 1940

Take Cover warning 10.50 am — 11.5 am

Off Duty. Slight gun fire. Clear skie. Saw many vapour rings and lines made by planes.

Take Cover warning 1.20 pm - 2.10 pm Off Duty. Battle over Dagenham Docks. Heard planes swooping. Many vapour rings. Sounded like several bombs dropped.   6.13 am Off Duty. Another all night raid. One of the heaviest we have had. Planes continually round this district. Press estimated over 200 planes came. Terrible disaster at Boulton Rd. And Stanhope Rd. At 7.50 pm a land mine exploded. The rumour is 3 killed and 60 odd injured. If so, it is nothing more than a miracle. There are about 70 to 80 houses untenable. Our door at 493 Becontree Ave was forced opened with blast breaking woodwork and lock catch, also shop fronts blown in ⅝ of a mile away. Hundreds of homes ruined after tiles had been shattered. Then very hard rain, my estimation is 12 to 13 hundred houses affected from severe, 15 slight, hundreds of ceilings down and partition walls. Hundreds of tillers at work. Small bomb fell in Warrington Rd 100 yds from four houses and several heavy bombs at Chadwell Heath. The total houses condemned is about 200. Two more have since died.

Reign of Terror 1940

Civil Defence

In every town there were Civil Defence Wardens, as mentioned earlier worked in shifts to be available in the event of air attack. They would help with clearing the debris and looking after the injured, after an occurrence. The picture below is one of the many East London Crews, this group from Ilford in 1940.

At the time there was a severe shortage of purpose-built ambulances and there was a need for more vehicles to help with the injured from the air raids, so civil vans and cars were used. The ambulance in the picture is nothing more than an elderly van called in to serve and probably had no more than stretchers with perhaps a medical kit in the rear of it. Because of the strict black out laws any form of light showing during the hours of darkness was forbidden. The man on the left who is leaning over the car headlight, note the cowling over the front of the light unit to prevent aircraft from seeing the vehicle at night, it also meant the driver could not see a great deal either. The other head light has a hood over it and the lens has been blanked out with a number on it, the wording says 'A CAR' which no doubt glowed at night and had some meaning to other rescuers.

Reign of Terror 1940

London certainly was not the only city to receive the attention from the German Bombers, whilst all the events were a horror in themselves, with flames burning out of control and beautiful and interesting buildings reduced to rubble, the difference was the bombing was not so prolonged as the event in the capital which suffered 176 nights of continuous bombing from September 1940 through to February 1941, after that period until May of that year it was not as unrelenting as before however, still heavy. Hitler having not achieved his objective of the surrender by the United Kingdom had turned his attention elsewhere.

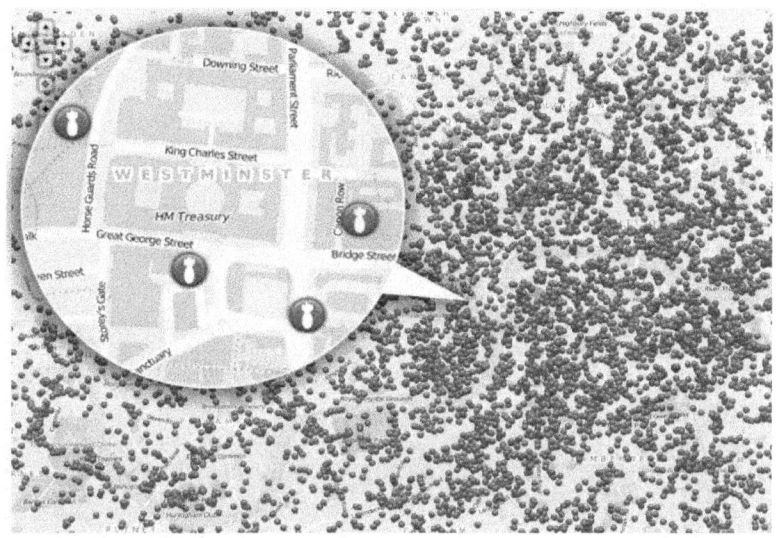

London where the bombs dropped with Westminster highlighted

Reign of Terror 1940

During my research into the history of that period it has shown that diverse parts of the country suffered very differently. As in this instance I am told of a story where the people who lived about twelve miles from the centre of Bristol, which was virtually destroyed, and yet they went through the war with only the inconvenience of rationing and shortages being a problem.

Following is a collection of events at different cities, they are in no particular order.

Sheffield

December 12th 1940

Somewhere in the higher echelons of the German Luftwaffe, orders were being prepared and sent out in coded messages to the numerous bomber units spread across occupied Northern France by the German forces. The ground crews would very quickly proceed to the area where line upon line of different types of explosive devices were stored. They would start to retrieve the deadly bombs and incendiaries, wheeling them on low trollies, arranging them so they could be loaded on to the hundreds of waiting aircraft who had received their lethal instructions to be prepared for an operation. Close by the Pilots and Engineers and other flyers who were to operate these deadly aviation machines would be standing in groups receiving their orders.

Sheffield is an old town which was named in the twelfth century after the River Sheaf that flowed below the castle that was built at that time. It still passes through the city although now most of it is out of sight in culverts below the metropolis's buildings, its route is to the North where it joins the river Don.

Most of the development changed the community into an industrial town took place in the Middle Ages, when it became part of the power house of the industrial revolution. Cutlery, which the town was to become internationally famous for was first produced in the sixteen hundreds. Another manufacture giving it worldwide recognition was Silver Plating invented in 1670, this was the ability of putting Silver onto copper for fancy goods and tableware, lowering the cost of production and mimicking the items made in the precious metal.

In the suburbs there were numerous factories close to the river Don, and since the start of the war countless of them had been altered from peace time merchandising and were producing items to help with bringing the deadly conflict to a close. One of these units 'Hadfields' was the only factory in the U.K. producing shells that could pierce eight-inch armour plating.

On a cold Thursday evening, December 12th, 1940, Sheffield was a busy place with its many industries humming in support of the war effort. The people, despite the severe shortages, were preparing for Christmas in their free time away from their employment, trudging from shop to shop, all of which had little produce on the shelves, searching for 'tit bits' to make the Festive Season more enjoyable, despite the war.

At Bletchley Park, in Gloucestershire, which had been developed as the nerve centre for code breaking, they were intercepting signals from Germany which were being sent to their forces with the code name *Schmelztiegel ("Crucible")* which indicated that the enemy were planning a large air raid. Frantically all facilities were deployed to decipher the message to specify where it was intended, they would have been aware that time was short.

(Editor's note: I have been trying to find out the significance of why the 'Crucible Theatre' built in Sheffield in 1970 was so called ... was it because of the code name used by the German forces?)

To the centre of Sheffield most of its buildings are the splendour of the Victorian period, it was a time when the town, as then, (it converted to a city in 1899), became very wealthy with the development of Iron works and similar facilities most of which were on the East side. On this evening its buildings, including the City Hall, with its many wide steps to the front, opened by Queen Victoria in 1884, stood in the fading light of a clear winter's day.

The thoroughfares full of traffic predominantly the horse drawn kind, trams on rails to the middle of the road, with overhead poles attached to swinging electric cables, as they were whining and clanging their way from stop to stop. Petrol or diesel was needed elsewhere so these types of vehicles were forbidden, there were exceptions, medical teams or those participating in the war effort.

In the bowels of the secret rooms monitoring events, operated by the British Security Services they became aware of radio beams (*German X Verfahren beams which were used by them so their bombers could follow the invisible emissions to a target*), were being laid from the continent across the North of the British Isles, and surmised the target was Sheffield,

Reign of Terror 1940

or another of the communities in the centre of the country. There was very little they could do to stop it.

There was a certain nervousness in the City of Sheffield as during the First World War German Zeppelins had bombed the city leaving 28 dead. So, precautions had been taken to minimise any repeat. But the new air onslaught would be nothing like the large air balloons of the previous raids of twenty odd years previously.

On that cold December evening, the War to the people in Sheffield seemed so far away, but for the restriction and the occasional attack by enemy planes little had changed. When the air raid warning siren sounded one wonders how they reacted, they had heard it many times before, some of which had only been practises … did they rush to the nearest shelter, or did they shrug their shoulders and carry on with what they were doing?

One thing is certain on that dreadful night they knew not what was in store and that their city would never be the same again.

A Heinkel Bomber

Reign of Terror 1940

The aircraft of the Reich had left the continent in large formations of 280 heavily laden bombers. The attack was made by three main groups of aircraft flying from Northern France. They flew across the North Sea crossing the coast above Skegness, and then a passage over the level lands of Lincolnshire before arriving at their target Sheffield, and the factories of the Atlas Steelworks, Brown

Bayley Steelworks, Meadowhall Iron Works, River Don Works, Darnall Wagon Works, Tinsley Park Collieries, East Hecla Works and Orgreave Coke Ovens., amongst others.

The whaling of the siren with their high and low sounding warning informing the public of the imminent attack. As it died away. Thirteen Heinkel 111s the pathfinder unit of the German group arrived over the city at 7:41 pm and dropped 16 SC50 high-explosive bombs, 1,009 B1 E1 ZA type incendiaries and 10,080 B1 E1 incendiaries. The first of these were dropped over the suburbs of Norton Lees and Gleadless.

Reign of Terror 1940

What was to follow that night was the destruction of the centre of the city. At about 9:30 pm a stick of bombs fell on Campo Lane and Vicar Lane, demolishing the West end of the Cathedral.

A t about 10:50 pm a 500 kg bomb fell on and destroyed the C&A and Burtons buildings opposite the Marples Hotel in Fitzalan Square.

The majority of the bombs on this night fell on the City Centre or on residential districts with the last bombs falling at 4 am. At 11:44 pm the Marples Hotel itself received a direct hit. It is not known exactly how many people were killed but approximately 70 bodies were recovered from the rubble. This was the single biggest loss of life in the attacks.

On the 15th December the raiders were back, this the second night of the Blitz saw the first use of a new German policy for their pathfinders. High-explosive bombs were no longer carried and were replaced by incendiaries.

Reign of Terror 1940

On this night the pathfinder force was made up of sixteen Heinkel 111s that dropped 11,520 B1 E1 incendiaries between 7 pm and 7:50 pm. The 15 large and numerous small fires started were visible from 90 miles away.

The main raid was carried out by 50 Heinkel 111s and 11 Dornier 17s. The raid finished at 10:15 pm. Many steelworks received hits, including Hadfields, Brown Bayleys and Steel, Peech and Tozer Ltd, although the damage was not serious enough to affect production.

In total over 660 people were killed, 1,500 injured and 40,000 made homeless. 3,000 homes were demolished with a further 3,000 badly damaged. A total of 78,000 homes received damage.

Six George Medals were awarded to citizens of Sheffield for their bravery during the raids. 134 victims of the raids were buried in a communal grave in City Road Cemetery.

King George VI and Queen Elizabeth toured the city soon after the raids to inspect the damage and boost morale amongst survivors.

Prime Minister Winston Churchill also toured the blitzed city, speaking through loudspeakers to a 20,000-strong crowd in Town Hall Square and giving his signature 'V' for 'Victory' V sign

Reign of Terror 1940

Prime Minister Whinstone Churchill's Speeches

Editor's Note: *Sir Winston Churchill, throughout his life was not one to be shy in what he said and was not one to mince his words. In the following extract from one of his speeches in 1942 whilst the words are of aggression it should be remembered at that time the British had suffered badly by the attackers, and many of its cities were in ruin. In London alone one in three houses had been destroyed in a six months period. All of the ports had been badly damaged whilst Coventry had all but been demolished with many of its buildings having received direct hits. There was a need for strong talk to boost morale in the people, which at that stage of the War was crucial and it is known the Prime Minister was very aware of this. His words were more for uplifting the spirit than a communication that was threatening.*

"The growing power of the British bomber force is the herald of what Germany will receive city by city from now on ... German cities, harbours and centres of war production will be subject to an ordeal the like of which has never been experienced by any country in continuity, severity or magnitude".

Extract from Winston Churchill, Prime Ministers Speech in June 1942

Reign of Terror 1940

The following is a discussion between a boy and his grandfather, a ninety-year-old, about his life and his memories of the war. It is surprising how the horror of the period has dimmed in the old man's mind.

As requested the names have been changed.

As told to Richard Seal

Marcus always enjoyed it when his grandad came to stay with the family for a few days. He carried an essence of innate warmth in every chuckle, a sense of profound comfort wrapped up in his dark brown voice, and the scent of cigar smoke and liquorice all-sorts. The man was always interesting to talk to, he had a lot of stories and loved to reminiscence, but he was also keen to dwell on the present moment and discuss the future. Moreover, he sounded genuinely interested in the life, thoughts and feelings of his oldest grandson.

Reign of Terror 1940

The teenager stared at his grandad in wonder over afternoon tea, as he reflected on what the elderly man must have experienced during his long life. It was difficult for Marcus to imagine being born way back in 1934 - what must it have been like for young Joe growing up during the black and white world of the 1940s and 1950s? The lad had come into the world just two months after the new millennium had begun, and he had turned fourteen on the same day that the senior citizen reached the advanced age of eighty.

Grandad smiled at Marcus as he offered him a second cup from the flowery teapot. "I can imagine what you're thinking. Let me just say that I feel incredibly privileged to have survived for eight decades. It has been so wonderful. "

"What was it like growing up during the war, Grandad? It must have been scary." The young man loved asking about the man's early years.

"Well, we didn't think about it too much at the time, to be honest. I remember my childhood years with such fondness, there was a lot of fun to be had. Even school was okay most of the time. A lot of the young teachers ended up joining the army as the war progressed, while the older masters loved to show us maps of the British Empire. Our territories were coloured red, and they certainly seemed to cover a wide area!"

"The map of the World has changed a lot since then, hasn't it?"

"I'll say! Things have moved on, and we need to travel with the times."

Reign of Terror 1940

"What about living with the fear of being bombed - I can't imagine what it must have been like having something like that hanging over you all the time."

"Actually, there was always a feeling of camaraderie, with your family, friends and the community in general. We were all in it together and looking out for each other, it's hard to explain but there was a kind of cheerful defiance, a resolute, never-say-die spirit which felt comforting and empowering in a way.

With regards to daily life, it was no bother carrying a gas mask to school or going down into the air raid shelter when the siren sounded. In fact, I had my very first kiss down there, with sweet
 Emma." The man blushed fleetingly. "It was a special moment never to be forgotten. We lost touch after the war. I hope she went on to have a long and happy life."

Marcus's smile suddenly turned into a frown. "It must have been so tough with food rationing in those days, though. We

Reign of Terror 1940

have so many choices and luxuries these days, people are so spoilt."

"It was a way of life for everyone, we got used to the situation, and I must say we really appreciated a nice piece of cheese or meat especially when there wasn't much of it around. People would grow their own food of course. Dad loved spending time on his allotment, he was so proud of it. I helped him down there sometimes, digging and planting things in the fresh air. He used to bring home loads of fresh vegetables - I especially loved his green beans and carrots, and some of the potatoes were enormous! Our dear mother could work wonders with very few ingredients too, my sisters and I certainly never went hungry. She preferred not to have my help in the kitchen, though. More of the dishes seemed to get broken than washed under my watch!"

Marcus laughed. "It must seem strange to see all the fast food that we have now nowadays, lots of people are so fat." The lad shook his head, sadly.

"Let me tell you about the street party on VE Day! I've never seen anything quite like it ever since. Everybody seemed to be seized by an overwhelming sense of liberation, it was so funny seeing all the adults singing and dancing with each other, behaving like uninhibited children. I've kept the essence of the joy that I felt that night to this day."

"It must have been incredible. What did you and your friends like to do in your free time during those years?"

"We spent a lot of time outside, of course, playing football or cricket, and riding our bikes and so on. Naturally most of my memories involve long summer days, rather than miserable

Reign of Terror 1940

winter ones! However, my favourite activity was most definitely going to the cinema."

"Really? Did you go there a lot?" Marcus noticed the man brightening even further as he talked about this topic.

"Whenever I could. The local Odeon was always packed, and there were two different film programmes every week. I didn't mind whether I went there with mum, my best friend Pete, or alone to be honest. It was a popular form of entertainment in those days, but for me it offered a thrilling slice of magical escapism, so much more exciting than listening to the radio at home." The man drifted into his own thoughts for a moment, before continuing. "Do you like going to the pictures, Marcus?"

"Yes, I do. It's fun, especially seeing a good comedy or horror film with a group of friends, but it's so expensive these days. It's easier to watch at home, there is so much available online."

"Of course, technology opens up so many previously undreamed-of possibilities. You know, even when I was a

Reign of Terror 1940

child I realised that moments from my favourite films would continue to be touchstones throughout my life; this has proved to be true, and now I can revisit those classic scenes whenever I want to. It's marvellous!"

The teenager was struck by the man's infectious positivity, and undiminished zest for life. "Age isn't a barrier, Marcus, unless you want it to be. Senior citizens may have a wealth of life experience, but many don't appreciate how they can benefit from spending time with younger people."

Marcus felt flattered. "In what way?"

"The energy, passion and fun of youth is a joy to behold. I can't deny that ageing is difficult sometimes, but we must never forget how hard it can be to be young too: the peer pressure, exam anxiety, nagging doubts, endless uncertainty, conflicting expectations, crippling embarrassment and fear."

"It seems like you remember it very well!"

"Vividly! However, you'll never really get old if you have fun, a grateful heart, joyful spirit, and retain a sense of humour and willingness to laugh at yourself." He grinned at the lad. "Perhaps you'll have a conversation like this with your grandson one day."

"I really hope so!"

The man put his cup down and rubbed his hands together gleefully. "Okay, now please show me your new smartphone. I would like a demonstration of all the latest applications."

Reign of Terror 1940

We move on another city which sustained serious damage and was all but destroyed. However, unlike the capital city of London where the bombing was a nightly occurrence, the opposite happened, and the attacks were carried out over a very short period of time.

Coventry

No device or defence could save Coventry on the night of November 14th 1940. Three main forces of bombers screamed in over Lincolnshire, Portland and Dungeness, 439 of them, dark droning dots in the sky all heading for Coventry's and its arms factories.

It had become known earlier in the day that the Germans were planning something big for the North of England. However, their 'Enigma machine' (*See the story of the machine on page 142.*) had been sending coded messages to the Luftwaffe under the name of *Monddlichtsonate* (*Moonlight Sonata*) although received at Bletchley Park, Cheltenham, code centre it was not deciphered in time to be able to alert or save the city.

Coventry was an important engineering and manufacturing city before World War Two and the factories based there played a significant part in supplying Britain's military in the early months of the war.

Amongst the many industrial units there were 'Alvis' who made armoured cars while 'Aero' manufactured vital parts for the Royal Air Force. The workforce making these parts lived close to the factories and the bombing had a serious impact on their homes.

The Luftwaffe had made a very thorough reconnaissance of the city and knew where the key factories were. Planning for the raid on Coventry was equally as thorough as the Luftwaffe planned to be as destructive as was possible. Their plan was for an east to west flight over the city followed by a west to east attack.

The intention was to create a firestorm that would destroy factories and totally break the morale of the people. The ultimate aim of the attack was to

Reign of Terror 1940

create such a feeling of shock that the government would sue for peace.

Despite its importance as a manufacturing centre, Coventry was poorly defended against an aerial attack. Less than 40 anti-aircraft guns surrounded the city along with about 50 barrage balloons. One of the unofficial reasons put forward for this lack of defence was that the city was built in a geological dip which it was believed gave the area a natural defence against an aerial attack at night, especially in the colder months, the city was covered with fog.

The night of November 14th was very cold and also very clear as a result of the full moon. If it was true that the city's defences were kept at a minimum because of a nightly blanket covering of fog, it was not to be on this night.

The sirens first sounded in Coventry at 19.10. Pathfinder aircraft dropped parachute flares to mark the main targets. Incendiary bombs were

Reign of Terror 1940

dropped first. Many were booby-trapped so that when they exploded, hundreds of red-hot metal shards shot out. This first wave of bombings created over 200 fires.

At 21.30, the first high explosive bombs were dropped. They caused extensive damage. By 22.30 Coventry was effectively cut off from the outside, as very few phone lines had survived the bombing and travel was very dangerous as fallen buildings blocked the roads.

Not one German bomber was shot down despite thousands of anti-aircraft rounds being fired. Although one crashed, but no reason was given for it.

The only German bomber to crash

Quotations from residence at the time:

"We were all cowering on the floor – sheer terror."
(Ilene Bees)

Reign of Terror 1940

"You stood there petrified." Alan Hartley, ARP messenger during the raid.

"First reaction was shock. The second reaction was 'we're not going to let those buggers get away with it." Jean Taylor.

During the raid and in the immediate aftermath, it is generally accepted that morale in the city came very close to collapsing.

The city's fire fighters had to fight the many fires with a limited water supply as most of the mains had been shattered in the attack.

By 23.50 the centuries old St Michael's Cathedral had been destroyed.

By 01.30 on November 15th, the flames were so intense they could be seen 100 miles away. It was a perfect target for the second wave of bombers that came in at that time.

Reign of Terror 1940

In total the bombing lasted for 13 hours. 500 tons of high explosive bombs were dropped along with 30,000 incendiaries.

Later that day a team from 'Mass Observation' got into the city. As official reporters it was expected that any commentary on their films would follow accepted party lines – 'lots of damage but the spirit of the people is high; bombing will never dull the British bulldog nature etc'.

However, in this instance, 'Mass Observation' reported that the city had suffered a "collective nervous breakdown". It was reported that the survivors in the city attacked firemen for failing to stop the fires (even though they could not) and that police officers were also attacked. The government was so angered by this failure to stir the nation's patriotism that it came close to taking over the BBC, which oversaw 'Mass Observation'.

By the time the attack was over,
75% of all buildings in the city were destroyed.
33% of all factories were wrecked
50% of all homes.

Most people had to exist without water, gas or electricity

While 'Mass Observation' had angered the government, it had spoken the truth. On the afternoon of November 15th, a rumour went round the city that a second attack was on the way. By night-time, 100,000 people had fled the city for the surrounding countryside.

Reign of Terror 1940

There can be little doubt that the city was on the verge of collapsing from a morale point of view. This is why the government was so angered by 'Mass Observation' – it feared that people in other cities might become distraught as a result of the belief that what had happened to Coventry might happen to their city.

Ilene Bees, who survived the bombing, remembered the "total despair" she and others felt within the city.

However, this whole mood of despair changed on November 16th when King George VI visited the city. Observers noted that within the space of a day

– and linked to the visit – the 'Bulldog Spirit' that Churchill wanted to capture was very much in evidence.

On November 20th, the first of two mass burials took place. In total 568 people were buried. While they were very sad and solemn affairs, people there noted an air of defiance, of not wanting to give in.

Within two weeks of the bombing some factories had opened up. While food kitchens appeared, the basics of life had been severely disrupted – water, gas and electricity. People in the city were offered evacuation. However, only 300 took up the offer. The rest decided to stay in their city.

Coventry Cathedral after the raid

Reign of Terror 1940

The clear weather allowed the Luftwaffe to film the attack on Coventry. These pictures were used in propaganda films in Nazi Germany and the Nazis created a new 'verb', 'to coventrate', which was their reference to the mass bombing of the city. In later years when the RAF and the USAAF bombed cities in Nazi Germany, they used the words 'coventration bombing' to describe their blanket bombing attacks.

From Riddiford's Diaries.

Tuesday October 15 1940

Take Cover warning 1 1.25 am — 1 1.50 am On Duty. Very quiet here.
Take Cover warning 12.35 pm — 1.20 pm On Duty. Slight gun fire.
Take Cover warning 2.30 pm 3.15 pm On Duty. Slight gun fire.
Take Cover warning 4.00 pm — 5.00 pm
On Duty. Bomb at Broad St. Dagenham two squads called out also to Vicarage Rd. [note above: Mrs Dorrington in Vicarage Rd killed]
Take Cover warning 7.25pm — 5.00 am
On Duty. Our squad called out to Ballards Rd Rylands Estate Dagenham. 3 houses blew to bits. 7 people buried underneath. 6 killed. One woman and 2 dogs brought out alive. Gas leaking electric wires and telephone in various parts. Helped to carry dead out. Planes over head. Guns splitting. Several fires London direction. Home 12.00.

Reign of Terror 1940

We return to the Horror of London
and this true story

As told by Bob Thomas (RIP) and written by Percy Chattey.
It was October 1932 and it was a great time for me, although I do not remember it at all as I entered the world and arrived at my mother and father's home in South East London, at a place called Peckham. My name is Robert Thomas and in those far off days the area we lived in was a close-knit row of terraced houses built in the Victorian period. Street upon street stretching over a large area, all very similar in shape with the front door leading straight off a narrow pavement running along the side of a cobbled street.

The one we lived in was what is known as a two up and two down ... that is two bedrooms upstairs and two small rooms on the ground floor. To the rear a small scullery although some people liked to call it a kitchen, a tiny walled yard with a brick-built cupboard like construction that housed the WC, beyond that a gate leading to the narrow back lane.

Our road was wider than the others on the estate and on the opposite side from our house was a row of shops some of which had been converted from the original construction of

Reign of Terror 1940

a dwelling. Almost opposite us was Harry's 'fish and chip' shop where, as a child, for a half penny you could buy a bag of crackling.

During most days there would be horse drawn wagons trundling down the street to bring goods and supplies to the range of shops, making the turning very busy as there were also people doing their daily shopping. Some of my friends would feed the horses as they waited to move on to the next drop, but it wasn't something I liked, they looked sad and mournful and I was a little nervous of them, especially the tall ones that hauled large black sacks of coal loaded on a giant flat truck being delivered to the various properties.

Most of the time with my young friends, who lived nearby, we would play in the back yards or the lane that ran at the back of our houses. We must have looked very scruffy in short trousers and untidy tops. I never knew what work my mother did. She never said. She would go out early in the morning and come back some time later looking tired. We did not see a great deal of my father, I was told he worked in the London Docks and would catch a tram in the morning and return the same way in the early evening, although some nights he would not come home at all.

The war started at the same time I attended Junior school in September 1939. It was a tall imposing red brick building with a black slate roof and a large time piece situated above the front entrance as if warning people not to be late. The school had been constructed at the end of our road and had been built around the same time as the houses. It was not far from our front door on the same side, beyond a low wide black steel panelled railway bridge which crossed our turning close to one end.

The noise from the trains as they travelled across the bridge and along the embankment that ran to the rear of our home

Reign of Terror 1940

was something we had got used to, and I guess also the smoke and the soot that issued from the chimneys, not only of the trains, but also the coal fires burning in each household.

Although there was a lot of talk about the war in our small community it did not seem to bother anyone, as we got on with our daily lives as if it did not exist. However, there were restrictions starting to be applied on food and a range of things, which created interest in what information was in the daily papers and on the BBC News.

It was the following year when things came to a climax of this quiet period. I was sitting my end of term's examination when the war changed, and the first bombs started to fall during the day time. At first, we were not affected as Germany was more intent on damaging our defences prior to a planned invasion by the German Army and their forces. Their landing barges were being lined up on the French coast for the event, and had been shown on the newsreel at the local cinema.

It was after the summer break when the war changed and I had returned to the classroom for my second year of learning in the higher establishment. Shortly after we had gone to bed that night we had been woken with the constant sound of gun fire from the small Royal Artillery Unit situated beside the railway line. Then came the first explosions and they sounded so very close. Father was not at home. Mother dragged me out of bed and we rushed down the stairs to squeeze into the cupboard beneath them.

The staircase in the house ran side to side in the middle of the property and parallel to the road. Each side of the wooden treads was a brick wall going from floor to ceiling to support it. The bombers came every night, the wailing of the air raid warning would start a hasty retreat to what was the

Reign of Terror 1940

only safe place in the house. Mum had made it more comfortable in the insignificant enclosed space. My position in a small uncomfortable bed at the narrow end where the steps started with my feet below them, which created enough room for mother to lay on the floor with her feet at my head. It did get very stuffy, so sometimes we would sit together with the door slightly open. There was not enough room for Dad, most of the time he was still at work or when he was home he was on night watch aiding with casualties and helping in the clearing up of the bomb damage. If he did stay the night, then he slept under the big wood table to the centre of the room. The larger houses had shelters either Morrison brick-built ones inside the property or something like an Anderson in the garden, I guess our house was too small for either.

Everybody, where able, tried to live as normal. Every morning I would get myself ready and go off to school, where the first thing with classmates who had also arrived early was to go around the playground and collect any shrapnel which had fallen over night, especially the sharp pieces.

One morning I was a little earlier than the others and there was an object in a flimsy box. It was bottle shaped and it was obvious there had been others with it. I thought what a prize far better than the bits of torn metal the other boys had

collected for souvenirs. I removed it from the box and hid it for the rest of the day. After school I took it home and placed it, standing upright on the mantel shelf as a surprise for my mother.

Reign of Terror 1940

I was proud of my find and when she came home the 'surprise' was far different to the one I had expected. She took one look at this strange bottle standing proud on her shelf and screamed. She pointed at it … her hand was shaking. She looked at me horrified. In a demanding quivering voice she said "Take that thing to the Police Station NOW!"

The Policeman wasn't very impressed either as I took it out of a paper bag and I put it on the counter. He moved very quickly, with me wondering what all the fuss was about. Leaving it where I had put it he pushed me into a rear room. It was some time later when the Bomb Squad arrived and It was explained to me that what I was handling was an unexploded incendiary (as in the picture) which should have detonated and sprayed liquid burning fuel from it.

Although I was severely reprimanded for what I had done it was soon forgotten. The war moved on and the Germans continued with their Blitz. It was now October and the bombing had not been interrupted, every night the reign of terror would be back to pour down on us. In many of the streets around us houses had disappeared and had been turned into rubble or had been badly damaged. The trains had stopped running as the railway lines had been breached by a warhead and men were busy repairing the damage. On that occasion the rear windows of our house had been blown in. Part of the school had been smashed and the roof was damaged and was letting in water where the slates were broken or missing, and rainwater flooded parts of the building when the weather was at its worst. The classrooms were rearranged and there were more of us to a class. As most of the young teachers had been called up to the Services others, who had retired years before, came back to run the institution.

Reign of Terror 1940

We, that is Mum and I, had often talked about leaving and going to stay with relations who lived in Wales where the war was less intense, although neighbours and others would often try and persuade Mum to go she did not want to leave father on his own. As already stated, he was still on War work in the Docks in London, and when he came home he would join others at night in their task of 'Air Raid Wardens' in helping others who were in trouble because of enemy activities, which meant that we did not see a great deal of him.

As the weeks and months passed the nightly bombing continued, it is not something you get used to, it was more like being numb to it. And so, it was one night. We had settled down in our makeshift shelter and were trying to sleep despite the noise outside. It occurred to both of us that the raid seemed to be a lot closer than on other occasions. The explosions were constant, with the house shaking violently a few times, making the plates rattle in the small kitchen.

The bombs would fall in a line and sometimes it was possible to follow the direction of them. We could hear the detonations getting closer. I crawled up in the limited space to where my mother was laying, and we held each other close. We heard the scream as the missile fell to earth. The noise was total. Ear shattering. Everything seemed to be moving - shaking - and collapsing around us.

Silence! Our ears slowly recovered from the noise. It was very quiet although the muffled sound of the outside activity continued as if it was far away. We lay together with dust and dirt in the air knowing the house had collapsed around us. Falling masonry could be heard, individual pieces dropping down. Then it stopped. We had been entombed in our safety hole. The door was wedged shut and impossible to move. Slowly the dust settled around us. Mother's leg was hurting

Reign of Terror 1940

because part of the wall where a few bricks from the supporting wall had become dislodged had fallen on to her.

It was a long time before we heard movement as if they were looking for us We could hear the sound of digging. We were both feeling cramped and stiff in the confined space and but for the bottle of cold tea mother had brought in the previous night we would have been very thirsty. Earlier I had felt my way around trying in the pitch black to find what was laying on my parent's legs, and managed to remove the heavy object, a brick, very much to her relief.

It came as some comfort as we could hear the digging getting nearer and we could hear our rescuers talking. Someone shouted, 'over here'. Mother called out to them in a croaky voice telling them where we were. Shortly after, and to our surprise, daylight flooded in through an opening. Surprise because time had meant nothing and we both thought it was still dark but it was nearer noon.

They got to Mother first and carried her out on a stretcher, I was shortly behind her. The daylight blinding my eyes. I squinted through and was surprised to see part of the kitchen looked the same and had survived where the rest of the house was non-existent.

Part of the road had been cleared and parked next to the rubble was an ambulance (an old van really). The street was unrecognisable, both sides either destroyed or badly damaged.

The railway bridge was only connected on one side, it sloped down and the other end was laying in the road. The explosive device which had done this dreadful deed causing so much damage, had been a direct hit on Harry's Fish and Chip shop. It was now an empty space, a hole filled with rubble. The buildings to either side had collapsed. Our side of the road

Reign of Terror 1940

was not much different, what had been a row of terraced houses was now a pile of wreckage caused by the blast.

Crowds had gathered around us offering warm drinks and brushing the brick dust from us, a doctor looked at Mum's legs and declared they were alright but badly bruised. There was only one thought I could not get out of my head if the bomber crew had pushed the released button a tiny of a fraction earlier that projectile would have demolished our house instead, and where would we be now?

I did not feel lucky I was distraught. Deep down I was angry. Why! My way of life had been destroyed by a person ... an enemy ... I did not know. Somehow, I knew it was something that could not be forgiven.

From Riddiford's Diaries.

Sunday December 8 1940

Take Cover warning 5.40 pm — 7.15 am
On Duty. No warning. Sat. Nearly 46 hours with not even a yellow warning. But a lull before the storm, as this was one of the worst nights. Almost continuous AA gunfire the whole night long. Our squad was called out to Raydons Rd. Two bombs fell in Becontree Ave 100 yds the other side of Bennetts Castle Lane. 3 people killed at Aldborough Rd, Dagenham. South Street Romford closed, terrible lots of damage ARP Depot hit. Cars smashed. 2 killed near Oldchurch Hospital.damage ARP Depot hit. Cars smashed. 2 killed near Oldchurch Hospital.

Reign of Terror 1940

Hull

Hull was a severely damaged British metropolis during the Second World War, with 95 percent of houses damaged. It was under air raid alert for 1,000 hours. Hull was the target of the first daylight raid of the war and the last piloted air raid on Britain.

The city of Hull is a thriving port on the East Coast of the country and came into the enemy's list to be destroyed as shown here by information recovered after the war.

German Federal Archives

Luftwaffe report (19 June 1941, (translated)

**OUR OBJECTIVE:
THE SUPPLY PORT OF HULL**

The British Port of Hull, with its multi-purpose dockyards, its wharves and its strategically important industrial sites – this was our target yet again today. Along with the other aircrews of our unit, we took off last night, having taken aboard the bomb load which we intended to deposit to good effect in the middle of the great dockyards.

*

Of a population of approximately 320,000 at the beginning of the war, in the region of 152,000 were made homeless as a result of the bombing and the destruction caused. Overall almost 1,200 people were killed and 3,000 injured by air raids.

More than 5,000 houses were destroyed including half of the city centre. Three hundred thousand square feet (280,000 m^2)

83

Reign of Terror 1940

of factory space, several oil and flour mills, the Riverside Quay and 27 churches, 14 schools or hospitals, 42 public houses and 8 cinemas ruined

.Only 6,000 out of 91,000 houses were undamaged at the end of the war. Despite the damage the port continued to function throughout the period.

Hull's first air-raid warning was at 02:45 on Monday 4 September 1939: as an 'air-raid yellow' all operational crews

were called to their posts.

An air raid on the oil depot east of Hull at Saltend caused a serious fire owing to ruptured fuel-storage tanks and five men were honoured with the George Medal for their bravery in containing the fire: two firemen: Jack Owen, and Clifford Turner; and three Saltend workers: George Archibald Howe, George Samuel Sewell, and William Sigsworth.

Bombing intensity increased in the early part of 1941. In February several attacks resulted in multiple casualties, with around 20 people killed.

Reign of Terror 1940

In March major raids took place on the nights of the 13/14, 14/15, and 18/19. The first large attack targeted the river Hull corridor with damage to paint businesses in Stoneferry. The second assault was on St Andrew's Dock. A public shelter in Bean Street nearby was hit by a parachute mine (also known as "naval mines") causing multiple deaths.

The third major raid lasted six hours, and resulted in nearly 100 deaths, bombs dropped over a wide area of Hull, with many of them also causing damage west of the river. On 31 March/1 April the City centre was targeted, with predominant use of parachute mines. From the beginning of March to April bombing resulted in 200 deaths.

Attacks continued in April, with a major attack taking place on the 15/16th focused on Alexandra Dock, additionally a parachute mine hit a public shelter resulting in over 4 deaths, further mine attacks took place on the two nights between 25 and 27 April – six people were killed by a mine hitting the Gipsyville estate.

During the attacks many well known buildings were damaged or destroyed including the department stores of Hammonds, Edwin Davis, and Thornton-Varley and other buildings in the commercial centre.

Reign of Terror 1940

On the docks the Riverside Quay was destroyed by fire, and major fires created at timber storage around the Hedon Road area.

The Rank Flour Mill was directly damaged, as was the bus depot, and the buildings of the Hull Corporation telephone system. In addition to the areas of concentration, bombs fell on sites across the whole town. Over 400 people were killed during the attack, with many casualties due to bombs hitting communal bomb shelters.

The anti-aircraft guns and searchlights of the Humber Gun Zone under 39th Anti-Aircraft Brigade struggled to defend the city against the onslaught, though they and the night fighters from RAF Kirton in Lindsey scored some successes. In one notable engagement on 8/9 May, Gunner Maycock in a searchlight detachment from 40th (Sherwood Foresters) Searchlight Regiment, Royal Artillery, aboard a river barge named *Clem*, brought down a low-flying Heinkel He 111 bomber with a light machine gun.

The practice of 'trekking' or travelling to the countryside to sleep in the fields when bombing was expected, had begun in

Reign of Terror 1940

the First World War and by 1941 an estimated third of the population were leaving the city at night.

Minor attacks continued approximately monthly until the end of the year, with serious bombing in the early morning of 18 August and the night of 31 August/1 September.

.— Norman Collier, Comedian, Hull, "We lived in the middle of an industrial area that was a regular target for German bombers. One night as we were all filing into the air raid shelter Mum dashed back into the house." "Where are you going, Mary," said Dad. "Back for my false teeth," she replied. "Come back here, the Germans are dropping bombs not meat pies," shouted Dad

Our next true story

comes from Blackmoor a small village which is North of Southampton. Clive Adlam was born and bred in the small community and was ten years old, when the conflict started.

He remembers incidents very clearly and with clever words paints a vivid picture of events of that time. The community, compared with people living in London and other cities, had a gentler War. However, like everyone who lived through that period they were affected badly.

Reign of Terror 1940

Blackmoor

SCHOOL DAYS 1939-1945 by Clive Adlam

I was just 10 years old when, at 11.00 a.m. on Sunday, September 3rd, 1939 I sat by our wireless set with the rest of my family listening to our Prime Minister, Neville Chamberlain, as he addressed the nation. In sombre tones he informed us that Germany had ignored our ultimatum to withdraw their troops from Poland and as a result, a state of war now existed between our country and Germany. In spite of Chamberlain's previous attempts to stay at peace with Germany and his well-documented 'Peace in our time' treaty with Germany, I believe most of us, including ten-year-old school children, were expecting that eventually war would come.

My father Captain Tom Adlam Headmaster of Blackmoor School was on the military reserve and left to join the Army

Reign of Terror 1940

that same day. Before he left he told our family that with Poland on one side, France on the other and the British Navy's control of the sea he was sure Germany would not be able to hold out for long. Such was the optimism in this country at that time. Little did we realise that it would be six long years, after the most terrible conflict the world had ever known, before he would return to his family and Blackmoor School.

Before long Blackmoor had a new Headmaster, Mr Olding. We soon discovered that school life would be rather different under his administration. The cane which had previously been kept as a background threat and only used occasionally for serious offences, suddenly sprang into daily use for relatively minor misdemeanours. Three strokes across each hand was the normal punishment 'six of the best'. Most boys will remember how difficult it was turning the door-handle as you left the room using just the base of your palms and not your badly bruised fingers. Dinner breaks and playtimes became much longer and discipline in general suffered. When Captain Adlam returned after the war as Lieutenant Colonel Adlam in 1945, one of his first actions was to lock the cane away for almost a year. Such had been its misuse over the previous six years that it had almost lost any meaning as a deterrent.

And how much of the war were the children aware of? Possibly more than the older generation might have imagined. We all knew the French Maginot line opposed the German Siegfried line on the border between the two countries. This we imagined would be where most of the war would be fought in a similar fashion to the trench warfare of 1914-18. How wrong we were!

We were also very aware that unlike the first world war,

Reign of Terror 1940

fought mainly on the ground and sea, this war would have a third dimension, war in the air. Before long we were all issued with gas masks, which came in three sizes, large, medium and small. These were to be our constant companions to be carried with us wherever we went throughout the war.

Next air-raid shelters were built alongside the relatively new Pack-house at the back of the school. Why these shelters were erected in such close proximity to the shed with its vast expanse of red roofing, an obviously inviting target for enemy bombers, is difficult to understand.

Blackout regulations were strictly enforced. No light was permitted to show from windows or doors, while car lights were reduced to a narrow strip across their centre. Even bicycle lamps were half painted over in black or had covers over their tops. Every night we hung large blankets from top to bottom of our rather large windows in the school house.

Food rationing was introduced in January 1940. Our weekly ration per person was butter 2oz, sugar 8oz and bacon or ham (not both) 4oz.

By the end of 1940 equally small quantities of tea, margarine cheese and cooking fat were added to the list. As the war progressed so did further rationing of confectionaries such as syrups and sweets, while eggs and milk were controlled which meant the quantities allowed might vary according to their availability. Apart from food, clothes were also rationed such were the shortages at this time with the ever-present threat of German U boats to our shipping.

These meagre rations were accepted by everyone at the time knowing that food was scarce and our servicemen must be supplied. Whether rationing would have been quite so readily accepted had we known that it would not end until 1954, nine years after the war had ended, is perhaps another question.

Every household religiously saved their pots of dripping and I remember after collecting our liberal supply of milk in a can from Eveley Farm we would often skim off the cream into a large jar, add a little salt and then shake vigorously for several minutes to produce butter to supplement our ration.

Strangely I have no recollection of our teachers at Blackmoor ever discussing the war with us. The only occasion on which I recall any discussion was when we were visited by a government Post Office official who explained how we could help the war effort by purchasing National Savings Certificates.

We could buy shilling stamps on a regular weekly basis. These could be stuck into a savings book and after we had fifteen they could be exchanged for a certificate. He went on to explain that by saving in this way not only would we be helping the war effort, but the longer we left our money in savings the more it would increase in value. After his talk I

Reign of Terror 1940

remember raising my hand to ask a question. What would happen to our money if we lost the war? Rather taken aback he hastily replied that there was no need to worry because there was no possibility of that happening.

During the Autumn of 1939 Poland was quickly overrun by Germany from the West and Russia from the East. In France during this winter the situation remained relatively quiet. It was at about this time that we had our first air-raid warning heralded by the wavering note of the siren. Following the warning I remember our newly appointed 'Air Raid Warden' Jesse Buss riding his bicycle through the village furiously ringing a hand bell shouting at the top of his voice, 'Take cover, take cover!'.

Having carefully read all the Government pamphlets on what to do in case of air raids we gathered together in our front room, gas masks at the ready together with buckets of sand and water prepared for any gas or fire attack. It was something of an anti-climax when a short time later we heard the long steady note of the "all clear" and heard from the next news bulletin that enemy aircraft had been seen approaching the Thames Estuary. This had brought most of Southern England to a standstill. The lesson was quickly learnt and later sirens did not sound until enemy aircraft were in the near vicinity.

In the Spring of 1940 we were devastated when the German army attacked the neutral countries Holland and Belgium and with incredible speed swept through the Netherlands countries across France to the gates of Paris. The French Maginot line facing the German border, but not Belgium, proved utterly useless. At this point not only did France capitulate but Italy joined Germany to form the Axis powers.

Reign of Terror 1940

There followed the almost miraculous evacuation of our own British troops from Dunkirk after which we were suddenly on our own.

We had no doubt that it would be our turn next to try to halt the seemingly invincible German army. Our Post Office official's assurance that there was no possibility of losing the war was not looking too good at this moment!

With the fall of France evacuation of children from London together with many other towns and cities commenced in earnest. Blackmoor House The Earl of Selborne's home, became the home of St Michael's Girls School from Worthing, although I remember seeing very little of them in the village.

Almost without being aware of it a gradual change took place on the farm. As men were called for duty into the armed forces so they were replaced by girls in the newly formed Women's Land Army, easily recognisable by their uniforms with green sweaters, brown breeches and broad brimmed hats.

Reign of Terror 1940

The Government called for Local Defence Volunteers and the LDV, which was later renamed the Home Guard. When formed it was not long before most of the remaining able bodied men in the village were recruited under the command of Lieutenant Snell, the local butcher from Pond End Cottages.

Next it seemed that almost overnight Blackmoor lost its iron rail fences including those by the Church cottages and the Vicarage walk, together with others from the Blackmoor road and round Blackmoor House gardens. This was apparently for recycling for the manufacture of armaments. After the war it was rumoured that the Government campaign to collect scrap iron was almost entirely propaganda, a morale boosting exercise with very little of it ever used. I hoped this was not true!

Nissen huts were erected in the woods behind the War Memorial and a cook house between the back of the school and the packing shed. These were soon filled with soldiers of the Pioneer Corps who we heard later went to Norway to help in their defence when Germany invaded both Norway and Denmark.

Reign of Terror 1940

At every opportunity we listened to our wireless sets for news of the war. Mostly we heard how our aircraft had flown over Germany and dropped leaflets urging the Germans to give up the war. Most of the school children considered this pathetic, wanting to hear how we had dropped bombs rather than leaflets. It occurs to me now that at this time the RAF was probably as short of bombs as the army was of rifles.

Suddenly we became aware of a voice in the background of our news broadcasts. It was William Joyce soon to be dubbed 'Lord Haw Haw' with his highly affected upper-class English accent. He repeated over and over how we were starving and should give up the struggle. His voice was rather faint and one of us would put an ear to the radio and repeat his words aloud. Far from lowering our morale we thought the whole thing absolutely hilarious even when he reported the troops stationed in Blackmoor would soon be obliterated by the Luftwaffe. Blackmoor had achieved world fame at last! Later it was rumoured that there was a German spy at Headley Mill from whom we assumed the Germans had received their information.

Back at school we embarked on the Government sponsored 'Dig for Victory' campaign. Blackmoor school, always noted for including gardening in its syllabus, was able to demonstrate what it could do.

Reign of Terror 1940

Bushes and brambles were cleared from the common land next to our school gardens after which we double dug as much as we could to plant potatoes. The grass lawn in front of the school was also turned over to the production of potatoes. Where the potatoes went after harvesting I have no idea. There were no school dinners at that time. When my father Tom Adlam returned after the war in 1945 his reaction was not good. There was his lawn so carefully nurtured for many years turned over to a potato patch! It took several years harder work to restore the lawn to its former standard.

Britain was now alone facing the might of Germany's Army and Air Force together with the U-Boat menace at sea the 'Battle of Britain' was about to commence. During the next two years there were regular 'dog fights' and air raids on Britain. In one daylight encounter I recall ducking behind the oak tree at the entrance to Eveley Farm, while two aircraft above were engaged in battle. The roar of their engines as they dived to and fro was punctuated by the rattle of machine gun fire. At night the sirens sounded and we could hear the quavering drone of enemy bombers passing overhead. When they returned heading south if they had any bombs left they would ditch them anywhere over the south of England before crossing the channel.

Reign of Terror 1940

During the blitz it was generally recognised that the safest place in any house was underneath the stairs. Bombed-out houses in London were clear evidence of this where stairways could be seen still standing in the midst of shattered houses. In our own house my mother cleared all the paraphernalia from our cupboard under the stairs and made a surprisingly comfortable bed inside where we slept for much of the time during the 'Battle of Britain'.

On two occasions during the night I recall the whistle of bombs descending on Blackmoor. On the first occasion the string of bombs stretched from Brockbridge to the common land behind the Vicarage. It was fortunate that no houses were hit, although I believe some windows in Blackmoor House were shattered. The next day I spent with Tony and Geoffrey Croft, the sons of our dairy farm manager, searching the craters for shrapnel. There were plenty of heavily twisted thick lumps of metal to be found scattered around, some of which we collected and took home for souvenirs.

On the second occasion one of the bombs landed in the field behind Upper Oakwood Cottages. This bomb failed to explode and, in an episode, closely resembling 'Dad's Army' the Home Guard dug it up, declared it to be a dud and built steps with a hand rail down the hole where the bomb was displayed for members of the public to view. Several prominent Blackmoor residents viewed and handled this bomb. It was extremely fortunate that it was in the middle of the night when not only did this 'dud' bomb explode blowing away both steps and rails, but also it shattered the windows and removed several roof tiles from Upper Oakwood Cottages. Had the bomb exploded during the day some of Blackmoor's subsequent history might well have changed.

Roy Lacey, a village farm worker, recollects in his memoirs how the Canadians in Bordon just 2 miles from Blackmoor, opened fire on five German Dorniers as they dropped their bombs on the camp. My brother Roger and I were in the Palace cinema at Bordon during this raid watching Greta Garbo in Anna Karenina The siren sounded the film stopped and the manager told us that enemy aircraft were overhead and we were to remain seated. We could hear both the pom-pom-pom of anti aircraft fire and the rattle of machine guns outside followed by the deafening explosions of bombs landing nearby shaking the cinema walls and ceiling. We were certainly frightened but to our relief nothing hit the building. The "all clear" eventually sounded and the film continued. As we sat watching, two young boys gave little thought to our mothers, who having witnessed the bombing and knowing where we were, both were near frantic with worry when we did not return home until two hours after the raid.

There was one further night raid on Bordon. The first wave of bombs missed their target but set the gorse and heather alight on the adjacent common. Seeing the flames from this heath fire the German air crews must have assumed the camp was on fire and proceeded to drop large numbers of incendiary bombs onto the common. As we watched, the night sky appeared to be rather like a bright moonlit night but with an added flickering reddish glow.

Reign of Terror 1940

All Britain's larger towns and cities had a protective barrage balloon network flying high above them during the war. These hydrogen filled balloons hung suspended by huge steel cables to prevent low level attacks by enemy aircraft. Occasionally one of these huge balloons would break free from its mooring to drift along wherever the wind might take it with steel cables ploughing through any obstruction in their path.

My sister Josephine recalls how she and her husband Bernard Swinstead, Blackmoors' Fruit Farm and Nursery manager, were woken early one morning in their house on Temple Hill by loud sharp cracking and snapping noises. Had the German invasion started or was it just another Home Guard exercise? Peering tentatively from a bedroom window they could see a barrage balloon. Incredibly enmeshed in its cable was a five bar farm gate tearing its way through the woods leaving a trail of broken trees and branches in its wake.

Possibly even more frightening was Benny Stennings experience when out in the middle of a field with his tractor he saw coming toward him another of these giant balloons. To make matters worse on this occasion there was not only a balloon, but also one of our own fighter aircraft attempting to shoot it down with Benny directly in the line of fire. Very quickly he abandoned his tractor as he ran for cover at the side of the field.

Inexplicably to us in June 1941 the Germans instead of invading England attacked Russia. It was generally believed that Russia was not particularly well armed and would soon collapse before the might of the German army. Had this happened, I am convinced the Germans would have turned their attention on this country.

Reign of Terror 1940

Fortunately for us and probably the world the Russians proved far stronger than anticipated by friend and foe alike, and we now had a rather improbable, but welcome ally in our fight with Nazi Germany.

By 1942 both my sisters had left home and my brother Roger now 18 had joined the RAF. My mother and I were now alone in the School House. The German bombardment

continued with regular raids, not only on London but on several of our larger towns and cities including Portsmouth and Southampton. During these raids watching from an upstairs window we could see a glow in the South and Southwest behind Noar Hill. At the same time we could also hear the rumble of heavy gunfire and bombs. Occasionally an enormous flash would illuminate the night sky. We were told these flashes were landmines dropped by the enemy. The whole thing was reminiscent of a distant continuous thunderstorm.

Later during the war the Germans became aware of our radar defence and dropped enormous quantities of string-like silver tinsel in an effort to disrupt the system. Whether this was successful or not I have no idea. There was plenty of it scattered in and around Blackmoor but radio broadcasts warned us not to touch it in case it might be contaminated.

When the Japanese attacked Pearl Harbour in December 1941 the Americans joined us in the war. The German raids continued in 1942 but by 1943 we witnessed a gradual change. The German bombing raids reduced to a minimum although air activity in the skies above increased enormously. We watched huge numbers of American four-engine Flying Fortresses and Liberator bombers covering the southern sky with vapour trails on their way to make daylight raids on Germany. These planes bristled with gun turrets with one of their major aims being to invite enemy fighter planes to try and stop them. At the same time our own four-engine Lancaster and Halifax bombers began to make their well-publicised thousand bomber raids. They also developed the art of hedge hopping daylight raids to avoid enemy radar and give anti-aircraft guns little time to target them.

Reign of Terror 1940

On two occasions these hedge hopping raids flew directly over Blackmoor. First they appeared as a myriad of small black dots covering the sky as far as it was possible to see from East to West. As they approached from the North over Blackmoor golf course and Eveley field they gradually increased in size until finally with a deafening crescendo of sound, literally causing the ground to tremble beneath our feet, these huge four-engine aircraft passed overhead at a height not far above the church spire. This was one of the most awe-inspiring sights I have ever seen. None of us who witnessed it will ever forget it.

The eventual end of the war with Germany came as something of an anti-climax. It was expected to end at a certain time on a certain date with Germany's unconditional surrender. It ended in this way but unlike the 1914-18 war which ended suddenly and unexpectedly I do not recall any mass celebrations. This may well have been because war with Japan still continued. To the children this war in the Far East seemed rather remote by comparison with the European war which had involved us all.

Reign of Terror 1940

Within two months, following the dropping of Atomic Bombs on Hiroshima and Nagasaki, the war in the Far East ended quickly and unexpectedly. This decisive weapon proving the ultimate horror of World War 2.

At peace after six years of bitter conflict we now found ourselves with a new problem, Prisoners of War. The camp in Drift Road was used to house Italians. With their arrival I recall the entrance suddenly transformed with swirling patterns of brightly coloured pebbles forming intricate mosaic pictures at the camp entrance. The contrast from the drab khaki and camouflage of our own troops, so necessary during the war, was incredible. Peace had truly arrived in glorious technicolour.

With our own troops still scattered from Europe to the Far East it took a long time for their return and demobilisation. In the meantime quite a number of the POWs were employed to work on the Estate at Blackmoor. When Blackmoor football club was resurrected soon after the war ended, no football league had been formed in 1945 and Blackmoor was fairing poorly in their friendly matches. It was then discovered that one of the Italian POW was a former International player who had played against England as centre forward in pre war years. We were pleased to accept him into our team and not only did our fortunes change dramatically but in our home games we had several hundred Italian POWS lining our touch line shouting, " Bravo il Curioni!"as they cheered their hero on.

With the war over how did I feel as a schoolboy during the conflict and looking back after some sixty years have passed, how do I feel now?

During the war there were certainly times when I was very frightened, listening to the high-pitched whistle of bombs descending nearby, wondering whether the next one would bring your last moments was not a pleasant experience.

In 1940 after the fall of France and during the Battle of Britain I certainly had a feeling of apprehension. How long would it be before we were invaded? What would it be like to see German soldiers marching through Blackmoor and occupying Bordon camp?

When to our surprise in 1941 the Germans attacked Russia and not England; suddenly we were no longer alone. When the German army failed to crush the Russians before winter set in to our astonishment they mounted a counter attack in the winter and the following spring. This was followed by victory of the British and Commonwealth forces in North Africa at the battle of El Alamein, I believe that at last we all felt a sense of optimism. The apparently invincible German army was not invincible after all! From this point onwards I never doubted, even as a schoolboy, that we would win the war.

In 1945 the Germans eventually surrendered unconditionally. Strangely I felt no great sense of elation. Had I been a few years older and involved in the fighting my feelings might have

Reign of Terror 1940

been different. As it was for six years there had been an undercurrent of excitement and sense of purpose. Internal squabbles and disagreements were put aside. We were all together as a nation with one overriding objective, to win the war.

Our leaders led by example. Party politics were dropped. The best brains in the country were recruited, regardless of party, to form a coalition government. We were all there to help each other and our country to stop the evil NAZI war machine and its attempt to dominate the entire European continent.

Suddenly with the war over it appeared at the time that a vacuum had been created. What would replace the sense of excitement and purpose? Would we retain the sense of comradeship which we had felt for so long? I did not know!
As I look back after more than eighty years my thoughts are rather different. Although it is no doubt true that war can bring out much of the better side of human nature, pulling together in the face of adversity and many acts of selfless heroism, I believe this plus side of war is far outweighed by the minuses, where the worst side of human nature is revealed.

I find it impossible to look back now without remembering the horrors of the NAZI concentration camps; not only were millions of Jews murdered but they were also starved and tortured until many of them resembled human skeletons. It was believed that the Germans took no Russian prisoners, there were no camps for them. And what happened to the thousands of German prisoners of war who vanished in Siberia? Little was said of this at the time. We can only imagine their fate. I can only echo my Father's words after he had taken part in two world wars - "War is undoubtedly a sickening business".

Reign of Terror 1940

Liverpool

Liverpool, Bootle complex were strategically very important locations during the Second World War. The Port of Liverpool had for many years been the United Kingdom's main link with North America, and would prove to be a key part in the British participation in the Battle of the Atlantic. As well as providing anchorage for naval ships from many nations, the port's quays and dockers would handle over 90 per cent of all the war material brought into Britain from abroad with some 75 million tons passing through its 11 miles (18 km) of quays. Liverpool was the eastern end of a Transatlantic chain of supplies from North America, without which Britain could not have pursued the war.

Merseyside

By Walter Dixon Scott, *Liverpool*, 1907

"It is a region, this seven-mile sequence of granite-lipped lagoons, which is invested ... with some conspicuous properties of romance; and yet its romance is never of just that quality one might perhaps expect ... Neither of the land nor of the sea, but possessing both the stability of the one and the constant flux of the other—too immense, too filled with the vastness of the outer, to carry any sense of human handicraft—this strange territory of the Docks seems, indeed, to form a kind of fifth element, a place charged with daemonic issues and daemonic silences, where men move like puzzled slaves, fretting under orders they cannot understand, fumbling with great forces that have long passed out of their control ..."

Reign of Terror 1940

This eight-hundred-year-old society which blossomed into a city in 1880. This marvel of originality and creativity, this district, one hundred- and seventy-six-miles North East of London on the Lancashire coast, constructed and developed on the banks of the River Mersey, which flows into the Irish sea.

During the nineteenth century its wealth surpassed that of London built on the trade passing through its granite and stone docks the first to be enclosed around the world and free from tidal movement.

In construction terms of major projects Liverpool has been the first in the globe for many developments, the first Rail link, the first tunnel under tidal waters and many more and of course the Merseybeat.

There is probably few souls in the world who does not know of 'The Cavern' where the 'Beatles' performed and were discovered. In the

Reign of Terror 1940

early sixties they stormed the World stage and became famous for their special kind of music. There were others at that time, 'Gerry and the Pacemakers' with their song 'Over the River Mersey' however, they were more famous for 'You'll Never Walk Alone' which became Liverpool Football Club's theme song. Besides others there was also Cilla Black renowned as a singer and TV personality.

However a mere twenty years before the heady days of the 'Rock and Roll' music created from this land of the Scouse ... the Liverpool Blitz was the heavy and sustained bombing of the city and its surrounding area by the German *Luftwaffe* in 1940.

Liverpool, similar to other towns and cities, was a heavily bombed area of the country, due to the city having, along with Birkenhead, the largest port on the west coast, also being of significant importance to the British war effort.

It was during one of these heavy raids and the city and the docks were being overwhelmed with various types of bombs and incendiaries, when one of the more serious single incidents occurred, a direct hit on an air-raid shelter in Durning Road, caused 166 fatalities. Winston Churchill described it as the "single worst incident of the war".

Reign of Terror 1940

The first major air raid on Liverpool took place in August 1940, when 160 bombers attacked the city on the night of 28th August. This assault continued over the next three nights, then regularly for the rest of the year. There were 50 raids on the city during this three-month period. Some of these were minor, comprising a few aircraft, taking place for a small period of time, with others comprising up to 300 aircraft and lasting over ten hours. On 18th September, 22 inmates at **Walton Jail** were killed when **high-explosive** bombs demolished a wing of the prison.

This pictures shows the bomb damage in Liverpool; Victoria Monument in foreground, the burned-out shell of the Custom House in middle distance

One very bad incident involved the SS *Malakand*, a ship carrying munitions which was berthed in the **Huskisson Dock**. It was a night when once more the enemy were doing its upmost to destroy the docks and the surrounding area. Close to the ship fires started in the sheds lined along the dock. A barrage balloon was burning and firemen and dockers were doing their best to douse the flames, but it was not possible, they spread to the *Malakand*. This inferno could not be contained. Despite valiant efforts by the fire brigade to bring the fire under control, it spread to the ship's cargo of 1,000 tons of bombs. They exploded a few hours after the raid had ended. The entire Huskisson No. 2 dock and the surrounding quays were destroyed, and four people were killed. The explosion was so violent that some pieces of the ship's hull plating were blasted into a park over 1 mile (1.6 km) away. It took seventy-four hours for the fire to burn out.

Reign of Terror 1940

A series of heavy raids took place in December 1940, referred to as the Christmas blitz, when 365 people were killed between 20th – 22nd December. The raids saw several instances of direct hits on air raid shelters; on 20 December 42 people died when a shelter was hit, while another 40 died when a bomb struck railway arches on Bentinck Street, where local people were sheltering. On 21st December another hit on a shelter killed 74 people.

The government hoped to hide from the Germans just how much damage had been inflicted upon the docks, so reports on the bombing were kept low-key.

Around 4,000 people were killed in the Merseyside area during the Blitz. This death toll was second only to London, which suffered 30,000 deaths by the end of the war.

This picture is looking towards the River Mersey

May 1941 saw a renewal of the air assault on the region; a seven-night bombardment that devastated the city. The first bombs landed at 22:15 on 1st May upon **Seacombe, Wallasey, Wirral,**

The peak of the bombing occurred from 1st – 7th May 1941. It involved 681 **Luftwaffe** bombers; 2,315 high explosive bombs and 119 other explosives such as **incendiaries** were dropped. The raids put 69 out of 144 cargo berths out of action and inflicted 2,895 casualties.

Liverpool Cathedral was hit by a high explosive bomb which pierced the roof of the south-east transept before being deflected

Reign of Terror 1940

by an inner brick wall and exploding mid-air, damaging many stained-glass windows. Another landed on the front steps without exploding but incendiaries destroyed equipment in the contractor's yard at the west end.

The seven-night bombardment resulted in over 6,500 homes being completely demolished and a further 190,000 damaged leaving 70,000 people homeless. 500 roads were closed to traffic as well as railways and tram lines being destroyed. 700 water mains and 80 sewers were damaged alongside gas, electricity and telephone services. On the night of the 3rd and 4th of May 9,000 workers from outside the city and 2,700 troops helped to remove debris

from streets, 400 fires were attended to by the fire brigade.

Bootle, to the north of the city, suffered heavy damage and loss of life. One notable incident here was a direct hit on a Co-op air raid shelter on the corner of Ash Street and Stanley Road. The exact total of casualties is unclear, though dozens of bodies were recovered and placed in a temporary mortuary which itself was later destroyed by incendiaries with over 180 corpses inside.

'The Times' reported that between the 31st March until April 13th, 1941" The Germans had stated that the attack on Liverpool and the surrounding area was one of the heaviest ever made by their Air Force on Britain. Several hundred bombers had been used,

visibility was good and docks and industrial works, storehouses and business centres, had been hit. In addition to many smaller fires, one conflagration, it was claimed, was greater than any hitherto observed during a night attack." (no doubt referring to the SS *Malakand*)

Today one of the most vivid symbols of the Liverpool Blitz is the burnt outer shell of St Luke's Church, located in the city centre, which was destroyed by an incendiary bomb on 5th May 1941. The church was gutted during the firebombing but remained standing and, in its prominent position in the city, was a stark reminder of what Liverpool and the surrounding area had endured. It eventually became a garden of remembrance to commemorate the thousands of local men, women and children who died as a result of the bombing of their city and region. Affectionately known as "The Bombed-Out Church" by the locals, St Luke's regularly hosts food and drink festivals, film screenings, art installations and many more events both in the ruins and in the surrounding garden.

Reign of Terror 1940

Children at Play
The Innocence of playing
in the Bomb Damage inflicted on Liverpool.
Told to and written by Richard Seal

My childhood growing up in Liverpool is dominated by vivid memories of the cold which seemed to be an ever-present feature and permeate every part of my skinny body. It felt as if the chill had enveloped my bones, and never fully left me, even during the summer.

While I, Jack is my name, wore long-sleeved shirts and jumpers during the winter months, they seemed to be pitifully thin, poor quality and no match for the harsh elements. Also, I was obliged to wear shorts all year round, my skin must have been tougher than old boots. Still, it was the same for all the children and no-one complained about such things in those days.

The family home was large, but it felt cramped as it was occupied by a lot of people. My older sister Janet and I shared a room at the top of the house and my parents had another, while my grandparents and Aunt Polly were on the ground floor.

There were always a number of family members around throughout my youth, so my parents did not assume particularly distinctive roles. Mum seemed to be so busy around the house, washing clothes, cooking and cleaning from morning until night, while dad was an elusive character who never said very much to anyone. He was at work most of the time, then went to fight in the war from which he was never to return.

We lived close to the port, which was a huge, bustling place. It seemed to be, and was busy, twenty-four hours a day with seagulls swirling around overhead heralding the boats which were constantly arriving with mysterious people

Reign of Terror 1940

from weird and wonderful places then leaving for strange, unknown destinations - perhaps dangerous, almost certainly exciting and exotic.

The people they carried seemed to either scuttle past with their bags, keeping their heads down, or strut around calling out to announce their presence. My father worked there for a while. I was later told that he was an electrical engineer, but to me it seemed like he must be an undercover agent doing some kind of espionage work for the Government.

As a child I loved visiting the countryside and going fishing with friends. I also enjoyed spending time helping on our large allotment nearby, feeling in touch with nature and animals. We grew fruit and vegetables, so we had a ready supply of fresh produce. I thrilled at the feeling of the potatoes' strong roots as I dug my fingers into the soil. Feeding the chickens and pigs was a wonderful way to disconnect, and I picked names for each one of them. When I was alone on the allotment, Harry the pig would listen without judgement as I shared my stories, laughter and anxieties.

I could not contain my enthusiasm for playing sport, especially football. I was strong, lithe and fit and could run faster than everyone else. I loved athletics and had particular strengths in both sprinting and long distance running. I preferred to do physical things rather than stay at home reading or helping around the house like my sister.

I was particularly excited when my father, grandfather and some of the other men built a couple of bomb shelters for the local community. Whenever anything needed to be fetched, I would be more than happy to oblige and took off on my heels. I felt that I was as capable as the adults and was determined to do my bit wherever possible.

I had a lot of fun at the local school, especially when playing rough and tumble activities in the playground. There were no

Reign of Terror 1940

rules and plenty of scrapes and bruises whenever we played any kind of sport or games, but my overriding memory is of messing around and lots of laughter. I met my best friend and partner in crime Eric there and we spent so much time together both in and out of school.

I remember him as a dark, scruffy bundle of fun, a diminutive ball of hyperactive energy, always keen to play or explore. He was never introspective or low, and I felt re-energised whenever I was in his presence. I remember little about the lessons or teachers but enjoyed being away from the claustrophobic family home and constant reminders of war and hardship.

In the classroom Eric and I used to sit together and nudge each other, both repelled and fascinated by the sight and sound of the giggling girls huddled together. Blond, light blue-eyed Diana often used to stare at me, much to the amusement of her friends, and she would sometimes wink too. I sneaked a cheeky look at her now and then, returning her coy smile with a fleeting shy one of my own. This would sometimes be rewarded with a game of kiss-chase at lunchtime, Diana's long pigtails flailing as she chased me, and I ran at an appropriate pace to ensure I could be caught fairly quickly. I had to put on a show of distaste, but the look in her eyes suggested that it was not very convincing.

One day Eric and I were at a loose end, wandering down a lane by a canal, one of our favourite places. Idly sifting through a pile of debris next to the water we unearthed an interesting metal object. I immediately claimed this prize for myself, despite my friend protesting about his claim to joint ownership, because I had got it into my head that I wanted to remove its ring and wear it to impress everyone. For some reason, it never occurred to me that I might be handling an extremely dangerous grenade, and I was relentless in trying a range of methods to remove the

Reign of Terror 1940

ring. Hitting the thing with a hammer, kicking it and banging it against the wall did not do the trick.

In frustration, I discarded the grenade only to retrieve it again a few days later and resume and redouble my efforts. Eric would stand by and watch, making a helpful suggestion now and then, although he was lucky not to be in the vicinity when I managed to achieve my goal. I was incredibly fortunate not to be killed or badly injured as I had tossed it into the canal when the ring finally came free. There was a loud explosion with water cascading into the air. I did need to visit the hospital for some minor shrapnel wounds on my arms and legs. I shudder to think of this incident now, but at the time it just felt like another lark to relieve the boredom and I shrugged it off without any further thought.

My happy school life came to an abrupt end one Sunday night in September, shortly after the new academic year had just begun. My classmates and I arrived on a sunny Monday morning to find that an enemy bomb had totally destroyed the building the night before. We all stood there looking around in disbelief at the scene of utter devastation. It was just the first of many such experiences during the course of the war, but I had no idea that I would not attend school for nearly a year after that incident.

At first the appearance of bomber planes was a terrifying spectacle, it felt like a malevolent force had been released from hell to unleash fire and fury on the unsuspecting city. However, we got so accustomed to the sound of their arrival almost every night that they eventually became a familiar feature of life's routine. At times it felt like we were almost desensitised to their fearsome presence and took the attacks for granted. When the port was bombed, the havoc wreaked was regarded with a quiet acceptance. My friends and I were disappointed that the local policemen discouraged us from investigating the site and taking souvenirs.

Reign of Terror 1940

However, my attitude to the experience of being bombed changed significantly on the terrible winter's night when Eric and his family were on the receiving end of a special delivery from the Luftwaffe. The explosion following the bombs' screeching, whining descent was so intense that it felt like our shelter was trying to wrench itself free of its foundations. The sound was deafening; I was shaken violently like an old rag doll for a few seconds, and my head seemed to keep spinning long after my body had stopped moving.

Amazed to find that we were still alive, the family tentatively ventured out of the shelter into a scene of grim, smoking ruin. Several houses had been damaged, some badly, but we stopped dead at the sight of the pile of grey and black rubble. My heart nearly stopped when I realised that this was Eric's shelter. There was an eerie silence in that slow-motion scene, as neighbours stood back with heads bowed, some covering their eyes with shaking hands. That empty silence still hangs heavily in a trembling corner of my soul.

I later learned that all that was found of Eric was his right arm, and his body was identified by the distinctive multi-coloured shirt that he was wearing. Earlier that day we had laughed together for many reasons, one of which being because we seemed to be the only ones with gaudy clothes, and we were both wearing the same blue and orange shirt. I still have mine at the bottom of a drawer, and I can see my friend's cheeky, grubby face in my mind's eye each time I come across it. That shirt stands as a reminder of the traumatic day that my childhood came to a premature end.

I have been living in retirement in Southern Spain for many years. The Hondon Valley, in the Alicante region, is an idyllic and tranquil place with abundant groves of oranges, lemons, almonds and olives. The views are stunning, the countryside is surrounded by mountains, and the climate is

Reign of Terror 1940

temperate all year round. It feels like a paradise on Earth, and I still sometimes find it hard to believe that I am living here. However, over the last year or so I have been feeling increasingly reflective, especially since turning eighty in June 2017.

    My childhood feels increasingly like the memories of someone else, the events could not be further from my life now, and I feel compelled to share them before they are lost forever. The only photograph that survives from my early years still stands on the living room mantelpiece. It is a picture of my father and I, taken by my mother. It was a beautiful summer's day and the two of us are standing together with wide sepia smiles beside the port. I like to think that Dad is still on a secret mission to this day and did not really vanish without trace in No Man's Land.

Reign of Terror 1940

Birmingham

On the night of 9th August 1940 the **Birmingham Blitz** started with the heavy bombing, by the Nazi German *Luftwaffe,* of the city and surrounding towns in central England.

On the first evening of the bombing, just five days after the devastating attack on nearby Coventry, the first major air raid was launched against Birmingham, when around 440 bombers attacked the city, killing 450 people and badly injuring 540.

Around 400 tons of high explosives were dropped during the raid, including 18 parachute mines. The raid turned out to be the most severe attack on Birmingham in the course of the war. A number of factories were badly damaged in the raid, including the Lucas Industries, GEC works and The Birmingham Small Arms Company

Throughout the remainder of that year the bombing continued in individual raids until 23rd April 1943.

Situated in the Midlands, Birmingham, England's most populous British city outside London, is an important industrial and manufacturing location.

Around 1,852 tons of bombs were dropped on Birmingham, making it the third most heavily bombed city in the United Kingdom in the Second World War, behind only London and Liverpool and as in the others, incendiaries were used to create massive infernos far too difficult to completely control.

Reign of Terror 1940

As with most provincial cities which were bombed during the Blitz, reports of the bombing were kept low key. Wartime censorship meant that Birmingham was not mentioned by name in contemporary news reports about the bombing, being referred to instead as a "Midland Town". This was done in order to keep the Germans from knowing the outcome of their raids.

Official figures state that 5,129 high explosive bombs and 48 parachute mines landed on the city, along with many thousands of incendiary bombs.

A severely bomb-damaged street in Aston Newtown

In total, 2,241 people were killed, and 3,010 seriously injured. A further 3,682 sustained lesser injuries. 12,391 houses, 302 factories and 239 other buildings were destroyed, with many more damaged.

On 13th August the aircraft factory in Castle Bromwich which produced Spitfires was attacked. Eleven bombs hit the main

Reign of Terror 1940

target causing significant damage. 7 people were killed, and 41 injured.

The roof of the Council House was damaged by fire, and on the 29th, St Philip's Cathedral suffered serious fire damage after being hit by an incendiary.

In November 1940, a series of heavy air raids on Birmingham took place. Between the 19th and 28th of that month around 800 people were killed and 2,345 injured, with 20,000 civilians made homeless.

New Street after bombing

A member of the Home Guard and one of the company's electricians were later awarded the George Medal for their bravery in helping the trapped workers. The following night 200 bombers returned for another heavy raid, dropping 118 tons of explosives and 9,500 incendiaries, causing widespread damage. The main bus depot in Hockley was among the buildings hit, destroying or damaging 100 vehicles. A third consecutive major raid followed on 21/22 November.

Reign of Terror 1940

During this eleven-hour raid, large numbers of incendiaries were dropped, starting over 600 fires. The water supply system was badly damaged by bombs, causing three fifths of the city to lose mains water supply, firefighters therefore had to draw water from the city's canals. Supporting fire brigades from across the country were drafted in to help, and the fires were eventually brought under control. Nevertheless, Birmingham's water supply remained in a critical state, only one fifth of the normal quantity would have been available if there had been another raid, leading the Regional Commissioner to comment "Birmingham will burn down if the *Luftwaffe* comes again tonight." However, there wasn't another raid that night, and this gave engineers time to repair the water mains.

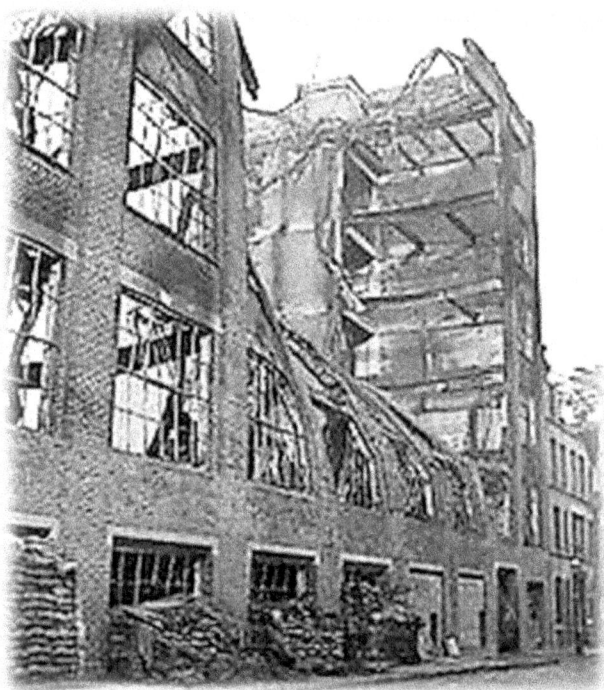

Around 60 bombers attacked Birmingham on 4th December. The Witton tram depot was badly damaged in this raid. One week later, on the night of 11th December another major raid involving 278 bombers was launched against the city. This

Reign of Terror 1940

was the longest raid of the Blitz lasting for 13 hours. Apart from explosives, around 25,000 incendiaries were dropped during the raid, causing widespread fires in both residential and industrial areas. 263 people were killed and 243 badly injured.

All but the fine tower and classical west portico of St Thomas' Church on Bath Row was destroyed in the raid. Its ruins now form part of St. Thomas' Peace Garden, a public park designated as a monument to peace and a memorial to all those killed in armed conflict.

Further heavy raids followed in 1941, on 11th March 135 bombers attacked the city. On 9th and 10th April, Birmingham was subjected to two heavy raids. In the first of these, 235 bombers dropped 280 tons of explosives and 40,000 incendiaries, concentrated on the city-centre. The Bull Ring, New Street, High Street, and Dale End all suffered heavy damage. St Martin in the Bull Ring was damaged and the Prince of Wales Theatre and Midland Arcade were destroyed.

Other areas including Small Heath, Aston and Nechells, also suffered heavy damage. On the second night, 245 bombers dropped 245 tonnes of explosives and 43,000 incendiaries, causing major damage in Solihull, Hall Green and Erdington. The two April raids caused 1,121 casualties. On the night of 16th May, another large raid caused damage to the Wolseley Motors factory, and the ICI factory. Although a navigation error meant that most of the bombers dropped their bombs on nearby Nuneaton by mistake.

The last significant raid on Birmingham came on 27th July 1942, when around 60 to 70 bombers attacked the city. The very last raid on the city came on 23rd April 1943 when just two bombs fell on Bordesley Green, causing slight injury, and the last air raid siren sounded on 15th May 1944.

Reign of Terror 1940

Important industrial targets

Name	Location	Production
Aerodrome Factory	Castle Bromwich	1,200+ Spitfires & Lancasters
Austin "Shadow Factory"	Longbridge	2,866 Fairey Battles, Hurricanes, Stirling's & Lancaster's
Austin Works	Longbridge	500 Military Vehicles/week
Rover	Solihull	Bristol Hercules Engines
Fisher and Ludlow	Birmingham	Lancaster Wings, Shell Casings, Bombs
Reynold	Birmingham	Spitfire Wing Spars, Light Alloy Tubing
GEC	Birmingham	Plastic Components
SU Carburettors	Birmingham	Aero-carburettors
Birmingham Small Arms Factory	Birmingham	Rifles, stem guns (100% of all made)

Other targets included: Dunlop - Chance Brothers - Lucas - Metro-Camel - Morris Commercial - British Timken - Hudson's - Whistles and the Monitor Radio Company.

Portsmouth

Reign of Terror 1940

Memories of a small child during World War Two.
Lucy Patricia Boby (nee Kneller)

I was born in Portsmouth January 1938, I was about 18 months old when war was declared in September 1939, my memories even from these tender years are so clear … I could talk from this time and was reading at the age of three.

The first time I knew things were different … why were the pretty curtains gone – big dark ones instead, and why didn't the street lamps outside our house twinkle at night anymore.

My Dad put a pink funny rubber thing over my head and I could see through a glass square in front, it had a funny tongue sticking out . I didn't like it at all. Mum said it was a Micky Mouse.! Later I learned it was called a Gas Mask, in case the Germans dropped gas bombs to hurt us … thankfully they never did. I didn't like Micky Mouse.

My Grandparents, Dad and an uncle owned a fruit and vegetable shop in an area of Portsmouth called Landport, they also farmed 100 acres of market garden with chicken and pigs about fifteen miles away at a place called Portchester. They were exempt from active service because they grew food for public use. Dad had a little 'Ford' lorry to transport the produce, despite the restriction of petrol at the time this little vehicle was heaven sent. When there was going to be a night air attack from the Luftwaffe, the Air Raid Wardens would let people know, and then Dad would literally pack family, friends and neighbours into the back of the lorry and drive them to the South Downs, Portsdown Hill, a segment of a range of hills running at the top of Portsmouth.

Reign of Terror 1940

In these hills there were tunnel shelters to protect against the bombs, these went into the chalk; and to my knowledge are still in place. Each family registered would receive a billet of two bunk beds also available were toilet facilities. Each family took its own blankets, food and water and the grownups tried to make it an adventure so we kids wouldn't be scared.

On one particular occasion, I remember although it was a cold, the night was clear and bright skies full of wonderful stars. There was a lot of people sitting on the grass outside the shelters looking down on Portsmouth. Through my young eyes the sky was filled with wonderful bonfires and a firework display and I could not understand why all the grown ups were crying and hugging each other ... even the men??? In later years I understood. Portsmouth was on fire!! It was January 1941 the Guildhall totally wrecked together with so much of our beloved city.

When I was about four, the warning siren sounded after three in the afternoon. Too early for a night raid. We were taken by Granny and Mum to a very sturdy brick shelter that stood in every street, but the closest to us was too full to let us in. So we hurried to another two streets away where there was room for our small group. Our men folk were still at the farm as it was harvest time.

As we waited suddenly there was a loud noise and a series of explosions and the shelter we were in, shook. We returned home four hours later ... our own shelter, which we had tried to get in earlier, had taken a direct hit. Fifty-Two people including six children were killed, people we loved, friends and neighbours all gone.

However, life went on, people were supporters of each other, shared food, handed out spare clothing ... beds were found if needed ... true comrades .

Reign of Terror 1940

I had lots of friends, one boy, Michael (head of our gang) he was just nine years old … would take us walking around the streets looking for shrapnel, he would sell it to a man he knew, and would give us kids 2p each. One morning he decided we would change direction, but another boy and I said, "let us go the normal way." We soon discovered why Michael had wanted to go another way, as there was a head laying in the gutter, and stuck on the wall of the Co-op Cake Shop, a pair of legs.

We became accustomed to bits of bodies, the resilience of children and were just interested in knowing if we knew them or if it was a man or lady.

One day my dad took me for a walk and we went to Commercial Road, a wide road and the main shopping area in Portsmouth. There were huge crowds, cheering and waving flags. Along came a band and hundreds of marching soldiers and sailors, I had a great view as I was sitting on Dad's back. Dad said, "look carefully now because here comes a very great man."

Reign of Terror 1940

Standing up in a jeep was a small man with a moustache, wearing a soldier's uniform and a black beret. It was Field Marshall Montgomery. These brave men were going across to France, sadly many casualties, but I was seeing the heroes of the D-Day Landings, and the beginning of the end of the War. It was June 1944.

Later, at the end ... street Parties, dancing, cheering, crying with joy ... jelly and custard, cake and lemonade.

Vivid memories of my childhood in war torn Portsmouth. So many to be able to write about, both happy and sad. I am thankful that my family remained safe, and the uncles who did go to war, returned safely. Surely, we all had Angels on our shoulders.

***

1943

Reign of Terror 1940

Four years into the War and Germany is starting to lose battles. However, it is still in control of the region with all the horrors as governor to the civilian population. The following is a piece written by *Lilly-Ella Mainstone*, a ten year old, for her English studies, the story is true and demonstrates some of the dreadfulness the inhabitant had to suffer…

The original of this work was inscribed in long hand - we have copied as written.

Annelies Frank

Annelies Frank is perhaps the most famous Jewish author across the world. She was born on the 12th July 1929, Frankfurt, Germany. Her parents were called Otto and Edith Frank, she also had an older sister named Margot Frank. It was the time of peace, before Hitler came to power in 1933. Before misery began.

Anne was an outgoing and curious child. She got into a lot of trouble at school far more than her quiet and serious older sister. Anne was more like her father whereas Margot was more like her shy mother. When Anne was four her father decided they should move to Amsterdam, because of Hitler plotting to capture all the Jewish people in Germany.

Growing up, Anne had lots of friends. She liked to play hopscotch, hide and seek, tag and bike racing. Anne got into a lot of trouble at school, her teachers nicknamed her 'mistress chatterbox.' The Nazi's invaded Poland in 1939 and the Netherlands in 1940 and left the Jews in danger. In July 1942, Anne and her family moved to a new hideout,

Reign of Terror 1940

they called it 'the secret annex.' For her 13th Birthday Anne received a diary from her parents and decided to call it 'Kitty.' She named it Kitty after a friend it reminded her of. Each diary entry; she wrote, 'Dear Kitty.' Anne wrote about all sorts of things, the first thing she wrote in it said, 'I hope you will be a great support and comfort to me.' The diary was green and red checked with gold edges.

Things continued to get worse, Hitler required that all Jews had to wear a yellow badge on their clothing. Some Jews were rounded to concentration camps. One day, a letter came through the post, it said Margot had to go to a labour camp. Otto was not going to let this happen. Otto and Edith decided to go to a new hideout, they told Anne and Margot to pack up their belongings and double up their clothing. Anne was upset as she wasn't allowed to bring her pet cat.

On the 6th July 1942, Anne and her family moved to a new hideout, 'the Secret annex,' but on the 5th July Margot had received a letter she had to report to the Nazi Political Police. Otto had been secretly preparing the Secret annex. Margot left first with Miep, the secretary, and then Anne and her parents left after them, so as there would be no suspicion. The annex had three small bedrooms, a tiny washroom and a large kitchen with a living room inside it. On the 13th July 1942 the Van Pels family joined the Frank family in the annex, they were also Jewish. The annex was behind a bookcase in a factory. Miep lived below and took food and clothes up to them.
On the morning of 24th June 1944, the Jews were captured. They were sent to Auschwitz Death Camp. A few weeks later

Reign of Terror 1940

the Franks and the Pels had to go to the Bergen-Belson Concentration camp, they travelled there by train. But the train was dark, cold and full of diseases. The camp was a horrible place and worse than the prison. Anne, Margot and Edith were split up with Otto. They didn't get any food and had to wear prison clothes, they had their hair cut really short, they had to walk bare foot everywhere on the hard ground and the Germans took away all their belongings. They slept in tiny tents on the floor.

Anne sadly died of Typhus, she will be remembered mostly by her diary.

Editor's Note

Anne didn't just keep a diary she also wrote tales which she planned to publish after the war, Otto Frank fulfilled her wish. Anne Franks Diary has been translated into more than seventy languages.

***

"Now those who sowed the wind are reaping the whirlwind".

Reign of Terror 1940

"There is no halting place at this point.
We have now reached a point
in the journey where there can be no pause.
We must go on."

Extract from Winston Churchill, Prime Ministers Speech in September 1943

A New Horror

Percy Chattey

A warm sunny day with its shadows lying across the ground, the soft wind rustling in the leaves of the trees, birds singing in the nearby hedgerows. Amongst this tranquillity the bowler paced out his run. Turning, he took a few quick steps and the cricket ball left his hand and whistled through the air, the cricketer lifts his bat ready to respond, swinging it making a solid hit, sending the ball to the boundary.

The boundary was the fence on the other side of The Close, a little turning off East Road. The fielders moved quickly to recover the ball as the batsman made a quick run to the other tree that lined the small turning, opposite the one that was used as a wicket. The ball was not really a cricket ball but an old tennis ball and the bat a shaped piece of wood, to suit the occasion.

In the summer, when everyone was talking about cricket scores or the results of some other game, we would make that sport the current pastime. There were no personalities back then, one side would be Australia the other England or maybe two football teams, whatever the current game was in the

Reign of Terror 1940

news.

As the seasons changed so did the professional games. Then the tree would become a goal post or maybe the home run for a game of rounders. It only needed imagination to change its function. Sometimes it was the finishing post for a race of self-built go-carts, (wheel barrows) made from pieces of wood and some old wheels normally from an ancient upright pram, with a length of string to steer the front ones which had been modified normally with a plank of wood with a nut and bolt to the centre so they would steer. If you were unlucky then you did the pushing.

If the machine you had spent many hours building, had no brakes then who cared? Putting your shoed foot on the front wheels had the same effect! Even greater fun if a wheel should come off and the driver fell out. It didn't really matter if you grazed your knee, hand or whatever; you got up brushed the offending part and started again.

I find it a little sad when I now see toddlers or children riding on factory built plastic toys, nowhere near the fun or education of building your own.

When we got bored with the carts or playing games around the tree then we would go for a cycle ride, but first you had to have a bike. There was no money to buy one and anyway because of the war they were not being made for home use as metal was required elsewhere. But somehow, we found them or bits of bikes which people had in their garden sheds and would happily part with the item. We lads would be busy gathering the pieces including spanners and screw drivers to build a cycle that could be ridden. A frame from somewhere – then a wheel and a chain- somebody would have a spare pair of handlebars and eventually one would have enough parts to make up a complete machine.

Schooling during the war, was a sort of hit and miss affair.

Reign of Terror 1940

Good young progressive teachers had been transferred to the armed forces, to do their part in the war effort. The authorities had to look elsewhere, and one of the answers was to bring back teachers who had retired. To our young eyes they looked really ancient. One thing was for certain, come rain, sun or snow, no matter how deep, school would be open and that is where you went.

Lessons did not follow a set formula, as teachers changed frequently. A maths lesson under one person could be learning the time tables; 2 x 2 = 4, 2 x 3 = 6, 2 x 4 = 8 and so on, perhaps repeating the full spectrum for the hour's lesson.

When it was time to have the subject again then another teacher would appear and maybe start teaching algebra, not at the start of basics but somewhere in the middle of a normal term lesson. All of which I, and I am sure others, found very confusing, not understanding the meaning of it at all. Sometimes just when you got into understanding what was being taught then it would be somebody else's turn to part with knowledge to a class of boys who were worried because of the war, or depressed because they had lost family or friends.

On another day, perhaps there would be no one who could teach the subject, so one of the supervisors would take us out into the playground to play hockey. In fact, I became very good at the game. Instead of hockey perhaps the instructor was used to teaching art so the lesson would change completely and we would spend the time painting or drawing

Reign of Terror 1940

.While the school was trying hard to give us an education it would sometimes be interrupted by an air raid warning. I have tried to remember where the shelters were at the school, I can remember lining up to go to them, I cannot say accurately where, although I think they were built of red brick in the playground. Perhaps because of the sheer terror of it, time has

blanked it out.

The Warren Boys Comprehensive School was to the east side of Whalebone Lane, with the playground to one side on the right. To the rear of the single-storey building was the girls section and beyond that farmed vegetable fields that sloped down to the town of Romford, which could be seen in the distance about three miles away.

One day we were playing outside during the break, when a shout went up, one of the lads had spotted a dog fight with fighter planes over Romford.

The playground extended down past the girls school, whose playtime was immediately after the boys. We were not allowed into the area where the females took their break, but I and a few others rushed down to look at what was going on. One of Germany's new horrors a V1 bomb, a Doodlebug, as shown, was flying over Romford heading for the fields and

Reign of Terror 1940

our school. These things flew in a straight line and were pilotless; the noise they made was a continuous drone.

There were two Spitfires chasing and swooping on to it, their guns firing in quick succession trying to shoot it down, or they would try and flip the bomb over by tipping one of its wings using their own wing to do it. My guess was so it would crash into the fields where it could only damage crops. They were not successful as suddenly the engine stopped and the Bug started to glide out of the sky.

We watched its descent and somewhere over to the left a mile or so away, a puff of smoke appeared, rising up from some buildings the sound of the explosion following a few seconds later. It was then we got shouted at by a member of staff for not only being in the girl's playground but for not taking shelter.

By now, after more than four years the war had taken its toll, with daily reports of people being injured or killed. It had become common place with little time for mourning, especially if you also had to find somewhere to live. On a number of occasions children had come into class crying after losing a loved one or sometimes they did not come at all, because they themselves had become victims.

On one occasion Dennis, who was a friend and sat next to me in class, was crying and full of tears all day, because his Father, a postman, had been killed that morning whilst delivering letters, when a doodlebug had hit the road where he was walking. All very sad but with no meaning to an onlooker – it was a long war, everywhere there were bombed out buildings and many a story of people being dead or injured. Somehow it started to have little significance.

In 1944 it was my brother's turn to go to Japan Road Infants School. *By now Japan was in the war and it became even more baffling why it was called Japan Road.* The hall in the centre of the primary school, with a large fireplace, had a high ceiling and was part of the roof, and in it a glass dome to let daylight in. Whilst my brother was having a lesson below this lighted area a V1's engine had stopped, there was a crash as it glided to earth. It had hit the glass of the sky light, showering the children below with splinters but luckily it did not explode, it continued its flight to where it destroyed the houses beside the park. The school was very lucky as no one was hurt.

The picture is the aftermath of a V-2 bomb at Battersea London, 27 January 1945 (from Wikipedia).

On another day in the afternoon, we were in class when we heard an explosion, it sounded very near. After a while one of the staff came into the classroom saying that the houses in East Road had been hit by a Doodlebug. "All those living in East Road put your hand up." Those who did, including me, were sent home.

I left the school, it was cloudy and overcast which fitted my

Reign of Terror 1940

mood, feeling very lonely, tears running down my cheeks and full of fear, and wondering what I would find when I arrived. When I turned into our turning I could see smoke and dust rising in the air from the far end of the road – thankfully our house was not affected.

I walked down to where the horror had landed. It had destroyed about four houses, some shops and the local doctor's surgery. The recovery people were still working in the wreckage moving bricks, wooden beams and other material trying to rescue the people buried underneath. The adjoining house of the group had lost its side wall - I stared up in shock looking at the upper storey of the building the floor was sloping down because of the loss of its support - the amazing thing the bedroom was still complete with bed, wardrobes and other furniture.

Worse was yet to come in 1944. We were at home when there was an huge explosion, I think, as I remember it was a Sunday as my parents were there. The ground shook with the house shuddering, again there had been no warning. It was the first of Hitler's new weapons to explode near us.

The V2 Rocket was a violent horror, many more times worse than the doodlebug, for it dropped out of the sky without warning. The power of its explosives was ten times that of a bomb. There was no noise, although some people said they heard a whistle before the explosion, but nowhere near long enough to be able to react and take cover. The bomb on that Sunday had landed in Chadwell Heath High Road destroying houses and shops.

This nasty weapon was the first type of rocket to go into space before descending on an unsuspecting public. It was the predecessor to the machines that went to the moon in the sixties.

Despite the fact that Germany was losing the war, as they were

Reign of Terror 1940

being overrun by the combined armies after the allied landings in June 1944, they continued to rain this high explosive device on the civilians in Southern England, and other places killing many thousands of people. It was a weapon that could not be accurately aimed at a target, so it was totally indiscriminate where it landed and exploded and what it destroyed and who was killed.

During the latter part of the war my Mother worked on the red trolley buses that ran out of Chadwell Heath, these vehicles were larger than normal buses carrying and seating over seventy people. From the terminus they went to various places. On one particular day Mum was the conductress in the rear of the bus collecting fares, they were on the way to Aldgate which is just outside the City of London.

The route followed the main road that runs from Essex, through Romford and the East End of London where it is known as the London Road. One day Mum was very late getting home and when she finally arrived, she was very stressed and tired.

It was a frightening story mother told, she had also been very lucky as she spoke of what happened. As the trolley bus was about halfway through its journey, approaching Forest Gate, where there is a major crossroads with traffic lights. On one corner the local telephone exchange also rows of shops on both sides of the road. Mum was collecting fares on the lower deck when suddenly there was a loud explosion. This large vehicle full of people on its two floors was blown on to its side.

The V2 rocket, again without warning, had demolished the centre of the town. Houses, rows of shops, a few pubs, the skating rink and the telephone exchange all reduced to a pile of rubble. If the bus that Mum was on had been a little further on its journey it too would have been reduced to nothing. This rocket was a wicked weapon to use against civilians, old or young, rich or poor it did not discriminate.

The people of East Road, at the top end where we lived, and the immediate houses around us, were very lucky as we came through it all with a few broken roof tiles from falling shrapnel, but I don't think there were any windows damaged, although I cannot say if other people from the street were hurt or injured elsewhere.

Code Breaking -
Enigma Machine

The Government Code and Cypher School, in 1938 was then based in London, and needed a safer home where its intelligence work could carry on unhindered by enemy air attacks. At a junction of major road, rail and teleprinter connections to all parts of the country and only fifty miles (80km) north-west of London Bletchley Park was eminently suitable.

Commanded by Alastair Denniston, the Park was given the cover name Station X, being the tenth of a large number of sites acquired by MI6 for its wartime operations.

The codebreakers arrived in earnest in August 1939. They masqueraded as 'Captain Ridley's Shooting Party' to disguise their true identity. It was to be the first instalment in one of the most remarkable stories of the Second World War.

Reign of Terror 1940

The Enigma cypher was the backbone of German military and intelligence communications. Invented in 1918, it was initially designed to secure banking communications, but achieved little success in that sphere. The German military, however, were quick to see its potential.

They thought it to be unbreakable, and not without good reason. Enigma's complexity was bewildering. The odds against anyone who did not know the settings being able to break Enigma were a staggering 150 million million million to one.

The Polish had broken Enigma in 1932, when the encoding machine was undergoing trials with the German Army,

Reign of Terror 1940

even managing to reconstruct a machine. At that time, the cypher altered only once every few months. With the advent of war, it changed to at least once a day, effectively locking the Poles out. But in July 1939, they had passed on their knowledge to the British and the French. This enabled the codebreakers to make critical progress in working out the order in which the keys were attached to the electrical circuits, a task that had been impossible without an Enigma machine in front of them.

Armed with this knowledge, the codebreakers were then able to exploit a chink in Enigma's armour. A fundamental design flaw meant that no letter could ever be encrypted as itself; an A in the original message, for example, could never appear as an A in the code. This gave the codebreakers a toehold. Errors in messages sent by tired, stressed or lazy German operators also gave clues.

In January 1940 came the first break into Enigma. There was a series of huts at Bletchley where the messages the enemy were broadcasting to their forces were received and were deciphered and turned into intelligence reports.

Their raw material came from the 'Y' Stations: a web of wireless intercept stations dotted around Britain and in a number of countries overseas. These stations listened in to the enemy's radio messages and sent them to Bletchley Park to be decoded and analysed.

To speed up the codebreaking process, the brilliant mathematician Alan Turing developed an idea originally proposed by Polish cryptanalysts. The result was the 'Bombe': an electro-mechanical machine that greatly reduced the odds, and thereby the time required, to break the daily-changing Enigma keys

The V1 Rocket

*The **Fieseler Fi 103**, better known as the **V-1** 'Buzz Bomb', (German: Vergeltungswaffe 1, retaliation weapon), also colloquially known in Britain as the 'Doodlebug', was an early pulse-jet-powered example of what would later be called a cruise missile. The V-1 was deve loped at Peenemünde Airfield by the German Luftwaffe during the Second World War. The first of the so-called Vergeltungswaffen series designed for terror bombing of London, the V-1 was fired from "ski" launch sites along the French (Pas-de-Calais) and Dutch coasts. The first V-1 was launched at London on 13 June 1944, one week after (and prompted by) the successful Allied landing in Europe. At its peak, over a hundred V-1s a day were fired at southeast England, 9,521 in total, decreasing in number as sites were overrun until October 1944, when the last V-1 site in range of Britain was overrun by Allied forces.*

Reign of Terror 1940

The V-2 Rocket

(German: Vergeltungswaffe *2, i.e. reprisal weapon 2), technical name A4, was a long-range ballistic missile that was developed at the beginning of the Second World War in Germany, specifically targeted at Belgium and sites in south-eastern England. The rocket was the world's first long-range combat-ballistic missile and first known human artefact to achieve sub-orbital spaceflight. It was the progenitor of all modern rockets, including those used by the United States and Soviet Union space programs, which gained access to the scientists and designs after the war.*

Over 3,000 V-2s were launched as military rockets by the German Wehrmacht against Allied targets during the war, mostly London and later Antwerp, resulting in the death of an estimated 7,250 military personnel and civilians.

Percychatteybooks
Story Telling (R)
Somerset House
6070 Birmingham Business Park
Birmingham
B37 7BF
Registered Number 2299335